South of Sixty

LIFE ON AN ANTARCTIC BASE

Michael Warr

D1319581

Antarctic Memories Publishing

Layout by Carol Fairhurst, Concept Design
Maps by Kelly Ruston, Spatial Mapping
Printed by Hignells Book Printing, Winnipeg

Antarctic Memories Publishing
Prince George, BC

www.antarcticmemoriespublishing.com

Library and Archives Canadian Cataloguing in Publication Data

Warr, Michael, 1943 –
    South of Sixty: life on an Antarctic base

    Includes bibliographical references
    ISBN 978-0-9738504-0-6 / 0-9738504-0-X

    1. Warr, Michael, 1943- 2. Antarctic Peninsula (Antarctic)—
Descriptions and Travel. 3. Outdoor life--Antarctic—Antarctic
Peninsula.
Title

G860.W37 2006   919.8"9   C2006-906816-7

Acknowledgements

I would like to thank the British Antarctic Survey, then only a year old when they signed me up, for the opportunity to first go to the Antarctic. Any thoughts, opinions, and mistakes in this book are entirely mine and not the Survey's. I thank those who were with me down south. We all grew from the experience.

For those who read the initial drafts, thank you. For W.D. West for photographs, Kelly for the maps and Carol for the layout, you were the greatest of help, as were Keith Holmes and Cliff Pearce who spent time on the so-called final draft. My daughter Julie I thank for the title. Finally, my gratitude is to the most important person, my wife Norma, who read the various drafts and gave unfailing critical support.

Introduction

Pulled by seven huskies, my rickety three-wheeled trolley bounced over the volcanic ash. Black cinders stretched to green Kroner Lake. Beyond, Port Foster's grey water was rippled by a moist wind. I was damp from the mist and rain. I had husky dogs, but was this Antarctica?

I had signed up as a meteorologist in 1963 with the British Antarctic Survey (BAS). With other young men I had sailed 8,000 miles from the UK to Deception Island in the Antarctic. Deception Island, the mouth of an old volcano, lay 60 miles off of the Antarctic Peninsula. The island was composed of volcanic rock, and half covered with glacial ice.

At Deception Island I worked and socialized with nine others, observed and recorded the weather, ran the Jesters, (the husky team), photographed seals and penguins, and visited the nearby Argentinean and Chilean bases.

My second winter spent further south at Adelaide Island was colder and brighter, with more wildlife, and another husky team. Glacier ice stretched from our base for ninety miles. There was no ash.

In *South of Sixty* I describe living on an Antarctic base. Most of us did not trek long distances across frozen wastes, nor did we camp out in blizzards for weeks on end. We carried out scientific work or supported that work at one place. Much of the time we cleared snow drifts, dug buried food boxes out of snow drifts, tended coal stoves, melted snow for water, fed and exercised huskies, and repaired our wooden buildings. We kept ourselves busy with photography, tobogganing, and skiing. Saturday nights were times for drinking, singing, and talking.

In my Adelaide Island year I sledged up the glacial island, and camped out in the snow on three occasions. Later I flew to 71° south in a Canadian De Haviland single propeller Otter.

On our bases we were isolated thousands of miles from home with no relief ships for eights months or more. Ten men lived in cramped quarters forced by severe weather and terrain to be dependent on each other. Emotions were generally kept under control, but there were occasional outbursts, especially after the darkest part of winter had passed. Harder still was having to leave the seclusion of the Antarctic after two years and return to the outside world.

The 1960's were a transition time towards today's more technical, more specialized, and more comfortable Antarctic life. Yet the Antarctic still constrains humans; it is the highest, driest, windiest, and coldest continent. Winter isolation is still a psychological and physical hardship, and humans still die in Antarctica.

In *South of Sixty's* final chapters I compared the Antarctic living conditions of forty years ago to the present when I visited the Antarctic Peninsula as a tourist. I had changed in the intervening years. The Antarctic had altered little; it still affected everyone who travelled to its icy landscape.

Some Antarctic Terms

Abseil - *descend a cliff on a climbing rope*
Avgas - *fuel for planes*
BAS - *British Antarctic Survey*
"Base B" - *British base on Deception Island*
Bergy bit - *floating lump of ice 3 to 15 feet above water*
Bog - *toilet*
Caldera - *a large collapsed volcanic crater*
Cloud levels - *cirrus:15,000 to 40,000 feet; alto: between 6,000
     and 20,000 feet; stratus: up to 6,000 feet*
Decepcion - *Argentinean base on Deception Island*
"Base F" - *British base at the Argentine Islands*
FIDASE - *Falkland Islands Dependencies Aerial Survey*
Fids - *long-term name for British Antarctic personnel*
Field - *away from the base*
Fumerole - *a crack discharging volcanic gas and steam*
Gash - *rubbish; "gash duty" is cleanup duty*
Grease Ice - *thin ice forming on top of the sea*
Growlers - *lumps of ice less than 3 feet in size above water*
Iceberg - *lumps of ice larger than 15 feet above water*
Katabatic - *wind moving down a slope at high speeds*
King dog - *dominant dog on a team; not always the lead dog*
Nacreous clouds - *rare luminous iridescent clouds; height 10 to
     15 miles*
Nunatak - *hill or mountain surrounded by ice*
Pemmican - *compressed dried meat*
Piedmont glacier - *broad ice mass flowing over a low-lying slope*
Sastrugi - *wind carved snow; like a ploughed field or worse*

Scree - *loose rocks on the side of a mountain*
Shelf ice - *ice attached to land, and projected out into the sea*
Skeds - *radio schedules*
Smoko - *a tea, coffee, food, or nicotine break*
Span - *heavy cable to chain huskies to*
"Base T" - *British base on Adelaide Island*
Tabular iceberg - *flat-topped iceberg broken off an ice shelf*
Tellurometer - *survey instrument that measures distance by
    reflecting microwaves*
Tidal crack - *gap between sea ice and land ice*
Tuff - *consolidated volcanic ash*
Valance - *flat strip around a tent on which boxes are piled to keep
    the tent in place*

Author's Notes:
Temperatures are kept at centigrade. Distances, wind speed,
weight, and altitude are in miles, knots, pounds, and feet, e.g.

   6 miles is approximately: *10 kilometres,*
   50 knots is approximately: *57 1/2 mph or + 92 kph*
   100 lbs is approximately: *45 1/2 kilograms,* and
   6,000 feet is approximately: *1,828 metres*

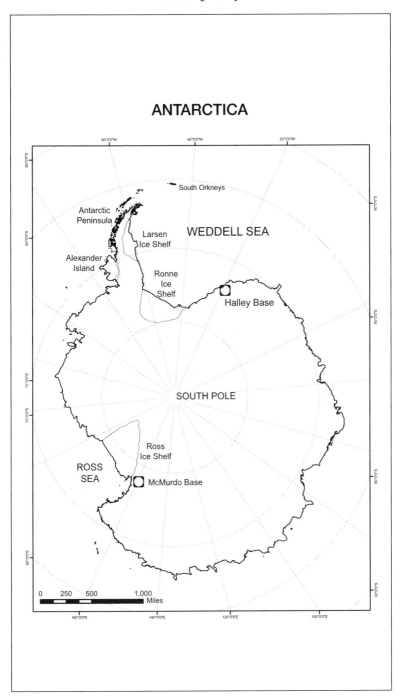

Contents

1

Antarctic Beginnings

I had never thought about the Antarctic before or after leaving secondary school. At school the careers master had frequently asked me: "Warr, what do you want to do when you leave school?" I had no idea. My marks in history and geography were not good enough to enter university. By default I drifted into Jackson and Warr, the London based family climbing, camping, and skiing store.

My father had started the outdoors business in the early 1950s. Apart from going up the outside of his block of flats he had never had the opportunity for real climbing. However, from companionable hiking with my mother in the Welsh mountains my father quickly surged off to a high level of rock climbing and mountaineering. In his late thirties he was making up for lost time.

An early family "holiday" had my father driving a motor-cycle through the rain, with my mother sitting behind him, and squabbling in the enclosed sidecar, my sister and I. We travelled to Saas Fee, Switzerland, so that my father could climb in the Alps. I have memories of camping in France near a sign pointing to "Les Roches," stringy cheese in soup, and high yellow limestone cliffs leaning over a road. We camped in a Swiss farmer's field, got yelled at for sliding down a luscious green grass slope, and waited for the mountaineers to return from above.

After an expedition to Svalbard (Spitsbergen) in 1954, my father's next endeavour in 1958 was to the Karakoram Mountains in northern Pakistan. The intention of the expedition was to climb Diran, an unclimbed peak of 23,800 feet. On a final push, Ted Warr and Chris Hoyte disappeared into cloud near the summit. They did not return. At age fifteen I watched a grown man cry as he gave the news of my father's death to my mother. I had been a bit in awe of my father, and at the time showed little outward emotion at his death.

Later on, like my father, I rock climbed. I slowly became my own person, but I still had no sense of purpose. In my second year at the store the new manager realized that I was not cut out for sales; the enthusiasm was lacking. He encouraged me to I apply to the British Antarctic Survey (BAS). I knew little of the Antarctic, but as I had no other goals in mind any change was welcome. Peter Daly's suggestion set me on a new course in life. If I had stayed in London my life would have taken a different turn.

Bill Sloman, the BAS personnel officer, stated I had not enough snow and ice experience to be a general assistant out in the field, and I was just twenty. Would I like to be a meteorologist instead?

"Sure!"

Five references were found attesting to my ability to live at an isolated Antarctic base, though until I was there it would be difficult to prove. Then I waited, not sure of what would happen.

Despite misspelling "shop assistant" I got signed on for two years with the British Antarctic Survey; I felt better. My climbing, camping, and skiing experience had helped. Only later did I realize how lucky I had been. In 1963 less than eighty or so new personnel went south to the British Antarctic bases. How many men had not been accepted? (British women did not get to winter in the Antarctic for another thirty years).

Basic medical checks were done. Other Antarctic organizations made sure their employees had their appendixes removed. This was something the British Antarctic Survey didn't insist on. There were fifteen new BAS meteorologists that year. Fourteen of us had never done any meteorology, but we did have a ten-week 'quickie' course. We had daily classes on how and what to note in the weather, we used meteorological instruments, and we had a regular ration of beer at lunchtime. Not having had the benefit of a university education I dutifully copied my colleague's bawdy songs such as "Eskimo Nell" and "Daniel In The Lion's Den." At the end of the course, Kenn Back, with a classics degree, and I were at the tail end in marks. Kenn ended up spending more winters in the British Antarctic than anyone else.

Later that summer all the new personnel spent a week at Cambridge for lectures on the Antarctic. At one session Bill Sloman had to read the riot act due to an overindulgence of lunchtime drinking by the men.

At home my mother was resigned to the fact that her eldest was leaving. By then I had started a bit of a social life, and often didn't tell her when I would arrive home. Years later my sister, Ann, reminded me that there was a lot of tension at our house at the time. She was preparing to go to a teacher college in South Wales, and never said anything at the time, but said I should have postponed my trip. My only concern was to leave home, and the Antarctic was my way of doing so. It was hard on my mother who had already lost her husband, but she said nothing. Perhaps she thought my being on an Antarctic base was safer than my plans to mountaineer in the Alps. Like most twenty-year old males I only considered my own needs.

2

Voyage South

On a Thursday in late September 1963, twenty-three men bound for the Antarctic met on a cold, damp Southampton dock. We were mostly young, on edge, and keen to be away from our families who had gathered around us.

Once we had stowed our luggage on board the RRS *Shackleton* and had sailed, we felt relieved and ready for anything. But the next day I wasn't ready for much. I was on clean up duty, (gash), and was interrupted every half-hour by being sick over the side into the grey English Channel.

Further on I had noted in my diary that the Bay of Biscay was as calm as the proverbial millpond. As we churned south at ten knots the sun shone, a robin perched on the bridge, and I now paid attention to the rainbow colours in the bow spray and the sound of water slopping in the anchor hole.

The first few days were spent getting to know the ship's personnel, especially the steward with whisky at six pennies a glass, and the other Fids on board. The general name for British Antarctic personnel was Fids. Before 1962 they had worked for the Falkland Islands Dependencies Survey so the name carried on. A solid wooden nautical tool is also called a fid. There are no similarities. Most Fids were in their early twenties. BAS preferred mature men, but they were generally otherwise engaged. The impressionable young men had to do.

Four of us bound for Deception Island in the Antarctic got acquainted. Len Mole, red haired and sociable, was from north England. Charles Howie, tall, dark and intense, was from Rhodesia. Don Parnell was relaxed, medium-sized, and from Manchester. I was tallish, thin, from north of London, and working on my social skills. There was to be a complete change of personnel at the Deception Island base. The shipping season was long enough there either to work out any personnel bugs, or to send people home if necessary.

The warmer weather brought out shorts and our tans. We raced beer cans down the deck, wrote diaries, did gash duty, played Scrabble, watched birds and sunsets, and took pictures. My Second World War German Leica 111c was being greased for a cold climate, and would be sent on later. Some Fids waited to choose a camera from the large selection of Japanese SLR models available in Stanley, the capital of the Falkland Islands, which had little tax, unlike Britain. I had bought 36 rolls of 24 Ektachrome slide film with me, or was it 24 rolls of 36? It just did me for the two years.

We enjoyed the cook's changing menu on the three-week voyage to Montevideo, Uruguay. It included melons, asparagus, herring roe, Dover sole, turbot, pork cutlets, gammon, chicken supreme, beef curry, spaghetti Bolognese, and duckling. Hundreds of flying fish glided in front of our bow; some managed thirty feet before re-entering the sea. One veteran Fid supplemented his diet with flying fish when they terminated their flights on deck.

Our duties on board were not arduous. We washed the deck, had the occasional fire and boat drill, and on Sundays we cleaned up before the captain's inspection; he was followed around by the first officer and an anxious looking steward.

The Fids took turns steering the *Shackleton*. The only time I saw Captain Turnbull get excited was when we passed a headland off one of the Madeira Islands. I was steering south when the captain ordered a turn to 240°. I forgot that the ship's momentum would turn us through yet another sixty degrees. There was a: "My God!" from the captain as we headed towards a line of rocks. He grabbed the steering wheel. There were some pointed comments by other Fids about the change in *Shackleton's* direction. The memory is still fresh.

The red and green *Shackleton*, less than a thousand tons, carried supplies and people to the bases along the Antarctic

Peninsula. The peninsula sticks out from the Antarctic like a hitchhiker's thumb in the direction of South America. The ship had a bit of concrete in the bow in case of *thin* sea ice. RRS *John Biscoe*, slightly larger and stronger, took other Fids further south to Marguerite Bay.

We talked about where we were from and what we had done, which for most of us was little. A third of us were down for two years in the Antarctic. The British Antarctic Survey liked the experience and thriftiness of having two-year people. Other countries only went with one year.

We discussed what we knew about the Antarctic. The goal-orientated Roald Amundsen reached the South Pole first in 1911 from the Ross Sea, and sacrificed forty-one of his fifty-five huskies to do so. We admired Robert Falcon Scott for his scientific emphasis, but not for the fact Edgar Evans, Titus Oates, Bill Wilson, Birdie Bowers, and he, man-hauled their sledges to the South Pole, and died on the way back. The weather had been unusually severe, but if Scott had taken the polar expert Fridtjof Nansen's advice and used dogs, he would have got his party back alive, though with little heroic status in Antarctic history.

The Fids admired Ernest Shackleton. In 1915 his ship, the *Endurance*, got crushed in the sea ice of the Weddell Sea. Shackleton's party of twenty-eight drifted on ice floes, and landed on Elephant Island more than a year later. From there six men, including Ernest Shackleton, sailed across 800 miles of the Southern Ocean to South Georgia in a small open boat. Shackleton, Captain Frank Wolsey, and Tom Crean then traversed unexplored glaciers and mountains on South Georgia in early winter to reach a whaling station on the other side of the island. All of Shackleton's men were rescued, though some did not survive the First World War.

Meanwhile on the *Shackleton*, we felt relaxed and hot; there was no air conditioning. We lazed in the sun, and slept out on the teak deck at night, as the temperature rose. I was still allowed to steer, although I got bored after thirty minutes. I read often, but not while steering. As we neared the equator the glistening flying fish increased in size, we got browner, and our bare feet hardened.

The heat produced great towering columns of dazzling white clouds that stood out against the blue sky. We would sail under a cloud, as it reared thousands of feet up, and for ten minutes we were soaked by rain. We were steam-dried on the other side. The ship's smells were warm salt water on hot metal and burnt diesel oil. As incipient Antarctic "explorers" we grew the mandatory beards. Did they hide the pimples or produce them?

Two weeks after departing the UK, the *Shackleton* stopped for five hours in the middle of the Atlantic to repair an oil leak. Two sharks appeared at the aft end, as did most of the Fids. A beef-baited hook brought a young four-foot brown and white-bellied shark onto the deck. Eric the cook dispatched it. Twenty-six pounds of shark steak was served for supper; it tasted like rich beef. Biologists extracted the upper-toothed jaw, and four suckerfish were preserved from the outside of the shark. A discharge of ship's oil scared off the companion shark and its striped pilot fish.

The next day was another full-page diary entry. The Crossing-the- Line ceremony was not something one volunteered for. We first-timers ignored the initial demands to come on deck. Joe Sutherland, the ship's Fid leader, dressed in elegant tin cans and petticoats, the 3rd officer attired as Queen Neptune, and Sparks as the chief crier, trooped around the ship. By early afternoon we were herded onto the aft deck.

The ceremony began with each person's crime and due punishment being read out to King Neptune, a.k.a. the captain. As I had been frequently sick in the English Channel I was administered twice with cod liver oil by the crewmembers. Others had an oral mixture of curry and pickles, and then brightly coloured liquids, grease, flour with cornflakes and feathers were poured over their unwilling heads. The victims were then thrown into a filthy canvas pool. A powerful hose was turned on us, which I turned back on the crew. I escaped further punishment by diving into the dirty pool.

Two mess-boys who had tried to hide were found, force fed, and dunked. Charles, an exempt official, avoided retaliation from the victims, by pouring the oral mixture away, but was still coated and hosed down. A general rush for the showers ensued. I carefully pulled the dyed dough out of my hair.

I kept my "Royal Decree" signed by His Majesty: Neptunius Rex and Master of the RRS *Shackleton* D. Turnbull: that in crossing "into our Southern Realm"... "He received due punishment for his trespass." The shiny golden bottle cap on a red tape and the red wax gave it an authentic look. Other more immediate equatorial reminders were a peeled back, and a headache if I stayed out in the sun too long. As a twenty-year old I learned by experience.

The sun now shone in the north. I found the sunsets impressive as the golden-red sun slipped quickly beneath the sea. At night I dreamed about the phosphorescent spots jumping among the waters of the bow.

The jokes on board got corny, as were the remarks about women and beer. I had no details except a "me also?" written in my diary.

In the middle of October four young wandering albatrosses joined our ship, their white bodies and black six-foot wingspan dipping past the crests of the waves. Other southern birds like the pigeon-sized black and white stippled cape pigeons appeared, as did porpoises. On board people were busy writing letters before we reached port. The Antarctic was still remote even though Fids watched colour slides of penguins, huskies, seals, sunsets, and icebergs. The present voyage was all that mattered. It ended in cloud, and greener waters as we entered Rio de la Plata. Black-backed gulls replaced the long-range sea birds. Islands lay on the starboard bow, and Uruguayan rock music boomed on the radio. We passed the resort town of Punta del Este, and dropped anchor at 10:30 at night one-mile offshore from a bright line of lights in Montevideo.

3

South American Indulgences

Montevideo was a welcome break to the long voyage. Apart from the need to fix the *Shackleton's* oil leak, we had to wait for aircraft parts required at Deception Island. We had the obligatory lecture on venereal disease from a ship's officer, and carefully placed the condoms in our wallets. Most never got used.

I have an old red stitched plastic wallet holding a variety of Uruguayan coins and grubby sticky paper money. There was no Proustian moment when I looked at the money decades later, but at the time Montevideo was our last oasis before two years of isolation, and we were ready to spend.

Montevideo's harbour curved away to the beaches in the east. The oil refineries lay to the west. The city spread up from the docks, where 200 unpaid-for British buses stood, to the centre near the impressively ornate red-bricked Victoria Plaza Hotel. We knew the few important Spanish words for beer, meat, and wine; for everything else we pointed.

The capital of Uruguay had more diversity than UK cities of the 1960's. Cadillacs were mixed with Model T-Fords, and modern concrete structures sat next to colourful turn of the century buildings. Toilets ranged from modern chrome flush types to pairs of footplates on either side of open drains.

The people were more varied than those in Britain at the time, ranging from dark skinned to fair European types, with a predominance of Spanish features and colouring. Dark haired, dark skinned, obviously wealthy men escorted young blond women through the downtown streets.

Whistle-blowing police stood in boxes in the middle of the crossroads trying to bring order to the confusion of vehicles. I found the police and military uniforms overly decorative compared to those back home. We weren't aware of the potential social and political troubles that lay ahead for Uruguay. We were just content with the now.

Unlike a British city on a Sunday, Montevideo was alive. Our first indulgence was a beefsteak eight-inches across and one inch thick, and at a third of the UK price. Next, like many of the Montevideo families, we attended the Sunday afternoon football game. The ball boys wore red tights, and transistor radios blared during the game. Around the field were strands of barbed wire, a concrete moat, and policemen. British football could have used some of these measures later on.

With some of the ship's officers, we started with expensive drinks at the Victoria Plaza Hotel, and then strolled back to the docks. At the "Anclar" bar we found cheaper drinks, various crew and Fids in different stages of inebriation, a steady roar of jukebox music, a small band, and prostitutes. The dockside bars were a contrast to the staid British pubs, and the beer was unusually cold.

Launches went back to the *Shackleton* at 8 in the morning (for the all-nighters), several times during the day, and the frequently used one o'clock in the morning departure. I kept myself on the edge of the drinking groups, and looked after the drunks. My drinking was limited. I wasn't ready to let go yet.

The next day after hastily mailing letters home and checking out a leather factory, Don, Tiny Norris (who was, of course, tall), and I took a side trip to Buenos Aires, Argentina. The PLUNA office arranged flights and accommodation for a total of six pounds each. We rushed back to the boat to get our passports, rushed to get a bus out to the airport, and then waited.

I was impressed by my first flight as we flew the 150 miles over the Rio de la Plata. Below, fluffy white cumulus clouds drifted along in the blue sky. An English businessman befriended us. He mentioned that Buenos Aires had the largest residential British population outside of the Commonwealth.

The Transocean Hotel was modern, and here I used my first bidet. We ambled along Florida, a crowded pedestrian street. Don didn't object when a pretty sales girl pulled him into a dentist shop, and sold him a toothbrush and toothpaste. In Buenos Aires the taxicabs were British, unlike the Mercedes used in Montevideo. The main boulevards were extremely wide and busy. The city had a more sophisticated feel to it than its Uruguayan neighbour.

The steaks tasted even better than those of Montevideo, though I miscalculated on how much money it would cost, and had visions of having to wash dishes.

We flew back early the next morning. At the Buenos Aires airport a busty air stewardess caught Don's eye: "You could see her before you could see her." My passport was now stamped for two South American countries.

Back at Montevideo we ate large plate-sized T-bone steaks at "Morini's." Joe informed us that Captain Turnbull was annoyed that we had not asked his permission to go to Argentina. It wouldn't have been forthcoming. We forgot that Fids, as "Falkland Islanders," were liable to two years military service under Argentinean law.

That evening a taxi took four of us to "Cubalette" where a doorman showed us into a darkly lit establishment. Thirty prostitutes lined the bar. We sat at a table, admired the dotted dice décor, drank the overpriced drinks, and looked at the ladies criss-crossing their legs.

Later at the "Anclar" at the docks, a well-known Fid barged past us saying: "Out of my way, I've just been fucked!" We let him go ahead. Most of us missed the one o'clock launch, and stood around on the dock in the cooling night. For a steep price four of us hired a boat back to the *Shackleton*.

The next day the agent forgot, possibly deliberately, to bring any money so most of us stayed on board. We sailed the following day in bright weather. I ended the day with my clothes spinning in the washing machine for seven hours. A vest and a tie had to be chucked.

4

The Falkland Islands

Our big city excitement lessened as we headed towards cooler latitudes, and green waves crashed over the plunging bow. The long distant sea birds had rejoined us. At 45° south we saw our first penguins. Penguins this far north were an indication of a colder than normal summer. We spend our time playing crib or bridge, and watching films of varying quality.

Four days after leaving Montevideo we docked at a wooden jetty projecting into the narrow Stanley Harbour. Low rolling grasslands surrounded the town of Stanley, which contained half of the Falkland Islands' 2,000 people. Stretched along military grid roads were rows of single story wooden houses clad with galvanized roofs. The town had three churches, and a few shops and hotels. There was one paved road. The rest of the island used rutted tracks that roamed cross the moors. Land Rovers were common, and boats and planes, necessary. Apart from the many penguins, the largest population on the Falklands was sheep.

The Falklands Islands lie 300 miles northeast from the southern tip of South America. The two larger islands, out of the several hundred, cover 4,700 square miles (roughly half the size of New Hampshire or Wales). The low-lying islands are deeply cut by long sounds. There is frequent rain, the temperature is mild, and the wind is a constant 15 knots.

John Davis, an English sea captain, first saw the islands in 1592. British, Spanish and Argentinean control of the Falklands flipped frequently until 1833 when the British took them over.

Argentina never forgot that the Islas Malvinas were theirs. In the 1960's the Falkland Island supply ship, the *Darwin*, used to spend four days travelling to Montevideo, rather than going to a nearby Argentinean port. The Falkland Islands were off South America, but not of South America.

The locals were called kelpers after the long strands of seaweed, and spoke with a West Country accent. The rest of the population were temporary professionals, and BAS people in transit. For the Fids, Stanley was a transition between urban life and Antarctic isolation, and on returning, a change from base life to civilization. The British Antarctic Survey used Stanley as its communication centre, supply base, and dispersion point.

In moist cool air, we humped bags of rock and sand onto the *Shackleton*. It felt good to be doing physical exercise. Around us mottled dolphin gulls, black-backed Dominican gulls, and giant grey-coloured petrels foraged in the water. The giant petrels, built like small albatrosses, paddled furiously to get airborne. They were timid and less noisy than the gulls. Nearby, flightless steamer ducks propelled themselves along through the water with a rapid circular motion of their small wings; flying was no longer necessary. Several blackened, derelict boats rotted along Stanley's half-mile wide inlet. The Falklands had been a final resting place for many sailing ships trying to weather Cape Horn.

Our stay in Stanley was indefinite. We awaited the *Darwin* and RRS *John Biscoe*, the other BAS ship. In grey weather we explored. Cannon pointed out towards the entrance to the harbour, and yellow gorse and daffodils bloomed. The few imported trees were bent by the perpetual wind. There were no native butterflies, land snails, reptiles, or amphibians. We strolled past the small cathedral in front of which stood an arch of the four jawbones taken from two blue whales. Each house had a stack of brown peat drying outside. The wind pulled sweet smoke from the chimneys. Stanley had a peaceful feel to it like the Outer Hebrides in Scotland.

Each of us had a short interview with the Governor of the Falklands; the Colonial Office oversaw the British Antarctic

Territories. The local BAS officials explained their role to us; London had been a little reticent on what Stanley did.

At the Falkland Islands Company (FIC) store there was a rush by Fids to buy up-to-date cameras. My purchase was a Swedish sealing knife; the BAS ones were not considered reliable enough. FIC controlled the islands' sheep economy, and owned land, the largest store, and the main transportation link in and out of the islands, the *Darwin*. Old money originally from the nineteenth century dominated the Falklands.

Our attention was refocused on the Antarctic when we each carried away from the BAS store two four-foot long stuffed duffle bags. Each bag weighed 30 lbs, and included, among other clothing, six pair of boots plus tall white mukluks, blankets, three colourful anoraks, (some hood-rimmed with wolverine fur, which did not freeze up), balaclavas, heavy and light gloves, sunglasses, underwear, socks, and a clothes repair kit (housewife). The cost to clothe each Fid was approximately a quarter of our yearly salary of 500 pounds sterling. We carefully tried on pieces of our clothing, but as we were not yet in the Antarctic we didn't over do it.

On the *Shackleton* we unbolted tables and chairs in the Fidery (our ward room) for a dance. Decorations and flags were placed around the room; one flag read "sex for all" nine times. Under the direction of Harry Rogers, a Fid cook destined for Halley Bay, we prepared food and drinks.

At the party I loosened up, and drank an assorted mixture of whisky, beer, and sherry. The girls who turned up were heavily out numbered. Coloured bulbs kept the packed and humid Fidery, dark. I was attracted to Margerie whom I had met earlier. I kept her close. This would be my last chance of female company for two years. However, I retired just after midnight.

Not surprisingly from the assorted drinks I had imbibed I had a headache the next day, and I received some ribbing for being so possessive of Margerie. I cleared my head with a walk up to the meteorological station above Stanley. Even on a calm day there was a breeze. In the harbour below gulls scavenged. Mussels were lifted into the air, and dropped onto rocks. The

SOUTH OF SIXTY

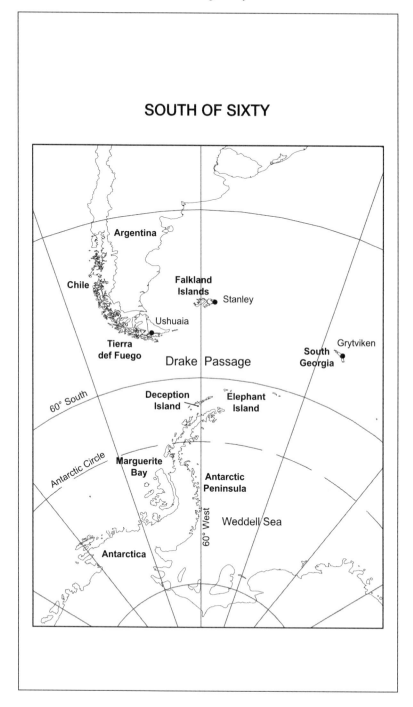

adult gulls croaked harshly; the young had a whining whistle. In the evening there was drinking at Ted Clapp's, the BAS organizer, and then we were off to a Halloween dance.

On the Saturday, John Noble, Tiny and I set off for a rock outcrop west of town. On the Two Sisters, Tiny and I did a severe rock route on multi-coloured lichen as rain fell. In thick cloud we used a compass to find Goat Ridge, further on. Close by lay stone "rivers" or bare stone runs, pushed up by ancient permafrost.

There was yet another party that night. I was tired, I had had too many drinking sessions too close together, I had enjoyed my climbing, and I wanted to get on with the job I was sent down for. I ignored Margerie, (regretted later), and retired early.

Another solitary walk the next day took me to Surf Bay. Under cool cloud, the bay displayed smooth sand and a half-mile wide belt of kelp offshore. I came across several red and yellow-breasted birds, jelly fish and star fish, and some recovering Fids. We gathered mussels to go with our duckling dinner.

On an excursion to Kidney Island north of Stanley, we struggled around six-foot high clumps of tussac grass. Most of the Falklands used to be covered with this tough grass before the arrival of humans and their farm animals. A large head peered through the grass. The bull sea lion was captured on film, and then "released." A smaller female avoided us by going around the other side of the clump. On this small island we found heron, oystercatchers, shags, turkey vultures, penguins, and kelp geese. The male kelp goose is pure white, and the female is black with a stippled breast.

The smell rather than the name gave Sea Lion Bay away. A large male sea lion with a small harem of two females inter-rupted us, and then lumbered off to the sea. More acrid smells and noise erupted at the rockhopper penguin rookery. The penguins had the usual black upper body and white front; the colouration made it harder for predators above and below to see them. Rockhoppers have a clump of yellow feathers sticking flat on either side of their heads. I have a picture of

Charles in a crouched position photographing a group of curious penguins. Both species were observing each other.

A quiet striated caracara observed us from a few feet away. They are rare dark hawks, locally called Johnny Rook, that scavenge for carrion, and don't mind humans. This had been their downfall. At present the Falkland Islands have the largest number of the 1,000 or so pairs left.

On our return we passed Sparrow Cove, and photographed the hulk of SS *Great Britain*. Built by Brunel and launched in 1843, she was twice as large as any iron passenger ship of the time. On her third voyage around the Horn, she was damaged, and joined other Falkland derelicts as a coal hulk. In 1970, the *Great Britain* was taken back to Bristol. When I saw her there in 1990 she had largely been restored.

In Stanley it drizzled again. The next day half of us were going to leave on the *Shackleton* for the colder South Georgia.

5

South Georgia and More Falklands

After the *Darwin* passengers, including two babies, moved onto the *Shackleton*, we departed in grey rain in an easterly direction. Followed by skimming cape pigeons and black-browed albatrosses we travelled the nine hundred miles to South Georgia in three days.

The first iceberg I saw was a sofa-sized growler that bumped along the hull making its tell-tell sound. Fids' cameras came out in earnest with the first large spiky iceberg even though it was five miles away. For me icebergs signified that I had arrived in the Antarctic. The last iceberg seen by me would mark my departure from the Antarctic.

In the distance, like a film backdrop there appeared from the dark grey sea, high snow-capped mountains stacked with wave clouds. South Georgia runs some 100 miles in a south-easterly direction, and is approximately 16 miles wide. It is deeply cut like the Falkland Islands, but under the Weddell Sea's frozen influence much of the island is permanently ice covered. There are more than 150 glaciers in deep fjords, and many rugged mountains with the highest being Mount Paget at 9,624 feet. The island is cold, wet, windy, and barren, and only near the coast is tussac grass found. There, thirty or so species of birds nest while elephant and fur seals bring up their young on the few beaches.

After Captain Cook took possession of South Georgia in 1775 the fur seals were killed for their skins. Later the elephant seals were killed for their blubber, which was rendered into oil. In 1904 permanent whaling stations were built on the island.

We came in opposite Grytviken, named by the Norwegians pot cove, a reminder of the rendering done for seal blubber. In cool sunshine and looking across at impressive snow-laden mountains, we Fids wore our yellow, green and orange anoraks. We felt one step closer to Antarctica.

The ship docked at King Edward Point. We walked over rocks and short tussac grass around to the Grytviken whaling station where three hundred Japanese workers processed whales. Two hundred and thirty two whales had been caught in the previous month of October. As we arrived a sixty-foot grey fin whale was being winched up on the sloping wooden plan.

The men's flensing knives cut a long slice down the side of the whale. Winches pulled off slabs of blubber and meat. Screaming mechanical saws cut up the bones. White intestines like giant sausages lay on the bloody wooden plan. Every part of the whale was used, and in thirty minutes there was no longer a whale except for the bloodstains on the plan. Behind the old rusty whaling station rose steep rock ridges, in the bay hundreds of cape pigeons squabbled for whale leftovers, and beyond lay the Japanese refrigerator ship waiting for the processed whale meat.

The next day in bright sunshine some of us got up early to pay our respects at Sir Ernest Shackleton's grave. A barely decipherable Japanese poem on a piece of rough wood lay in front of the grey gravestone.

I later led five Fids up the rocky triangular 1,900 foot Mt. Hodges. Amid a sharp wind we moved through patches of snow, and rotten loose rock. At the top, all around us lay peak after peak, some snow covered, others bare. In between were long white glaciers and rocky slopes. A long scree run, and a wet rear-end snow slide got us to the bottom.

I helped two Fids select wooden skis from the store: the price for the store man, a bottle of Teacher's Whisky per pair. In the afternoon we moved a hundred or so barrels of aviation gasoline (avgas). The tractor kept on digging holes for itself; once a shackle snapped and I flew backwards off the sled into the mud.

The large grey-coloured elephant seals were a South Georgia attraction. The males can weigh four tons, and be twenty feet long. The females are much smaller. At this time of year the larger males with their inflatable noses no longer had to protect their harems. The elephant seals lay quietly like giant grey slugs, snorting gently. Occasionally they opened a blood-red eye to observe you. When disturbed they made continuous belching sounds until the effort was too much and they collapsed with a sigh. Even when hunted earlier they saw no reason to move.

We journeyed back to Stanley in spitting rain and heaving seas. I heaved over the side as well. Two tiny petrels sat on a chair, and were fed bits of Dover sole. One, sitting facing inwards shot backwards, defecated over the side, and shot back to the middle of the chair. The next day they were launched off the ship. I felt better when after three days sailing we tied up at the Stanley government dock.

At Stanley we whiled away our time waiting for the *John Biscoe*. A wedding dance helped, but I needed a three-hour solitary walk to recover on the following day. Yorke Bay's long sandy beach was full of penguin prints from gentoos with a white slash on their heads, and the black and white striped Magellanics that brayed like donkeys. Overhead sailed the odd skua scavenging for dead penguins, eggs, or unattended chicks.

In the usual rain three of us later climbed slabs of gritstone above Sparrow Cove. Some of the rough grey rock was folded like blankets; other crags jutted out like ancient ruins. To the east lay long inlets and Kidney Island.

A previous rumour of the British reintroducing national military service was confirmed. The belief was that compulsory national service matured men though it was at the cost of much boredom. Unlike going to the Antarctic, there would be no choice. Maybe this confirmation explained the chaotic drinking that night with several broken glasses, maybe not.

The *John Biscoe* arrived with thirty more Fids, as did my refurbished Leica camera. Three of us moved on to the *Biscoe*, a more ungainly British built ship than the ex-Swedish *Shackleton*, but it was heavier and ice strengthened.

More Fids meant more parties. Doreen, a fifteen year old, favoured me. I wondered why I had attracted two of the few available young women. Was it good looks, being unattached, young looking and not liable to get them into trouble, or...? I certainly had thoughts on how to get Doreen into trouble.

The next day on a Mount Low trip with Charles, the immediate violent diarrhoea of "Stanley stomach," stopped any amorous thoughts. Charles explored as it drizzled, and did not complain too much about my condition. On the radio we heard that President Kennedy had been shot. I was not interested in an American incident thousands of miles away as I was centred on myself, and my liquid diet cooked over old berry branches.

I slowly got better. As we hiked we saw in the distance two hundred shags flying along Berkley Sound. Close by we observed a sheep with a broken leg, and a buzzard overhead observed us. Charles discovered two orchids. On returning to the *Biscoe* I drank only water at the cocktail party.

When the *Biscoe* left Stanley I again had the unpleasant mixture of gash duty and seasickness.

6

Finally, the Antarctic

We headed in a southwesterly direction across the six hundred mile Drake Passage with waves rolling eastwards. On a late November day, at two-thirty in the morning, I had recorded my meteorological observation in a rising wind. A storm roared out of the northwest at force 9 (winds of 47 to 54 miles a hour). The hatches were battened down. The Biscoe was turned away from her southerly bearing as huge walls of water swirled along the decks. No one managed to see the end of the exotic film, *The World of Suzie Wong*. The ship's corkscrew motions slid Fids up and down their bunks; we listened to the elements roar as the engines strained to keep the ship into the wind.

Two days later in calm waters we were off the northern tip of the Antarctic Peninsula in the South Shetland Islands. The peninsula is roughly a thousand miles long; the northern half averages 30 miles across. The Antarctic Peninsula is a snow and ice plateau, 4,000 to 6,000 feet high. Hundreds of glaciers cut into the plateau and move into the eastern Larsen Ice Shelf along the ice-bound Weddell Sea. On the western side, glaciers overhang massive cliffs, or calve into the sea ice. This ice breaks up during the few short summer months making the west side of the Antarctic Peninsula and its islands accessible by ships.

William Smith in October 1819 made the first recorded landing in the Antarctic on King George Island, South Shetlands. Sealers then nearly exterminated the fur seals in the surrounding islands. The Antarctic was then ignored for fifty years; there seemed to be a limited commercial potential.

There had been few explorations to the Antarctic in the nineteenth century. The Sixth International Geographic Congress of 1895 rekindled interest in scientific expeditions going south. The first was Adrien de Gerlache's Belgian expedition. In 1898 his ship, the *Belgica*, was trapped in the sea ice of the Bellinghausen Sea some 800 miles southwest of the South Shetland Islands for over a year. Two of his crew were Dr. Frederick Cook, who later claimed to have reached the North Pole, and Roald Amundsen, who was the first to reach the South Pole. The French explorer, Dr. Jean-Baptist Charcot, in two expeditions before 1910, mapped the Antarctic Peninsula down to Alexander Island, at the south end of Marguerite Bay.

Shore-based whaling started in the South Shetland Islands at the beginning of the twentieth century. Deception Island, where I was to spend a year, had a whaling factory until 1931. The Antarctic Peninsula continued to be explored, but not until Britain, Argentina, and Chile had all claimed the Antarctic Peninsula sector, around the Second World War, did political claims also become important.

After the war, military control of three British bases was turned over to the Falkland Islands Dependencies Survey. The three competing countries built more and more bases, hurled diplomatic notes between their capitals, and on one occasion bullets were fired. Antarctic base leaders would exchange formal letters of complaint, and follow this up with a friendly swapping of drinks and food. The International Geophysical Year of 1957 to 1958 produced scientific cooperation in the Antarctic, and the signing of the Antarctic Treaty of 1961 put all political claims in abeyance. The Antarctic emphasis was now on scientific research.

Our radar turned steadily as the *Biscoe* moved through shining white pack ice. The *Shackleton* tentatively followed as the ice split apart. The flat sea ice pushed back, and we stopped. A leopard seal and her pup looked on from a nearby floe. The *Shackleton* came along side, staving some of *Biscoe's* railings, to transfer aircraft parts and six Fids.

Shackleton headed back to Stanley whilst we re-entered the pack ice. In our bright, colourful new Antarctic clothing, Fids, loaded down with cameras, crowded the bow. As the *John Biscoe* pushed through floes, cracks radiated, and the ice rasped down the sides of the ship. The cold air had almost no salt smell to it. The sky was pale, and everything else was stark white. The red ship and the yellow, green and orange Fid anoraks were the only colours. Sun-goggled young men, barely managing to restrain themselves, casually walked from side to side photographing as they went, or nipped up to the bridge to check the position. As we moved slowly along, rounded floes crumpled at the edges. One had a line of unknown bird footprints arcing across it. The ship and the Fids' shadows lay silhouetted on larger floes. I used my father's Leica telephoto lens on distant birds and seals. Mount Pisgah, some 6,000 feet high on Smith Island, west of Deception, gleamed white in the sun.

On the last day of November we drifted with the pack ice. Crib and chess started up again; watching ice was passé. We cracked and crushed our way south through the last quarter mile towards open water into the Bransfield Strait. A loud cheer went up.

That night with almost no darkness we watched *The Birdman of Alcatraz*. Robert Stroud had died the previous week after serving 54 years in prison. He had made a decision as a young man that had cost him his freedom. We too had made decisions as young men to sign up for two years in the Antarctic. Hopefully our decisions were the correct ones. Once the ships left in a few months there would be no escape; we would be held for up to eight months at a time.

7

Our Deception Island Home

J*ohn Biscoe* moved past the black and white slopes of Deception Island. Like the American fur sealer Nathaniel Palmer, over one hundred and forty years before, we suddenly turned into the island through a 1,600-foot wide entrance. On either side of the narrow Neptunes Bellows were steep black volcanic cliffs. Inside the eight mile wide circular island was a magnificent natural harbour, Port Foster, some six miles long by four miles wide. Britain, Argentina, and Chile each had their own Antarctic base inside this small island. To quote *Richard II* Deception Island was "a precious stone set in the silver sea." Even though the Antarctic Treaty, signed in 1961, put Antarctic land claims in abeyance, possession was still politically important, especially for the safest harbour in the Antarctic.

The snow-covered hills of Deception were the remnants of a flooded caldera of an ancient volcano some twenty miles across. The two high points were Mount Pond at 1,778 feet and Mount Kirkwood at 1,505 feet. The rest of the rim was between 250 and 1,000 feet high, and averaged over a mile in width. The island was made of volcanic rock, ash, permanent glacial ice, and snow. This to me was not the expected icy wastes of Antarctica, but it was interesting, and it would be my home for at least a year.

Our ship anchored in Whalers Bay, a small bay off Port Foster. Brendan Lynch, the base leader, boated out to collect the first mail of the season. For the base members, visitors were less important than the news from home. We on board had the obligatory booze up; we'd arrived in Antarctica. I was content.

In a little wind and sun the Fids started unloading a year's supply of food for the base. Wooden boxes were placed in a net, craned up, loaded into a scow, and taken to shore. There was time to look at my Antarctic home. A black ash beach, more than a mile long, swept from the dark four hundred foot high Cathedral Crags past the wooden base hut to Kroner Lake. The almost perfectly circular green-blue lake contrasted in colour with the nearby grey-blue sea; it was several degrees warmer than nearby Port Foster. The base hut was sited a hundred yards up from the shoreline. Behind it, snow-covered ridges ran up to the summit of Mt Pond.

To the right of the base were the now disused Norwegian Hektor whaling station and a whalers' graveyard. Rusty oil tanks, broken machinery, and open-roofed buildings had slowly collapsed into the black sand. There was no sign of where the shore subsided and the buildings had sunk when the sea boiled in 1921, or the fifteen-foot drop of the sea floor in 1930. In 1842 volcanic fires had been seen on one side of the island. In 1945 hills 1,000 feet high were 8° C warmer than the surrounding air temperature. All we could see now was that at low tide the beaches steamed. If you put your hand into the sand it would be scalded. But at the time we had stores to unload, and I was too focussed on being in the Antarctic to have any concerns.

We unloaded thirty tons of boxes on to the beach over the next five days. A farm tractor dragged the supplies up to the base building. Breakables such as bottles of beer were carefully placed inside the hut. There was little initial inter-action between the newly arrived Fids with shiny new clothes and skimpy beards and the grubby seasoned Fids with luxurious beards. The priority was unloading the ship. Pleasantries would come later.

Biscoe House, my home for the coming year, was a long, dark, wooden-planked building that faced south onto Whalers Bay. Inside the hut ran a narrow corridor, lined with upright skis. The passageway smelled of creosoted wood, cooked food,

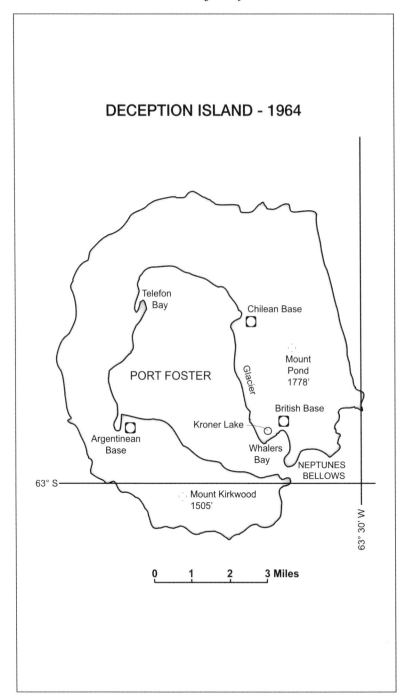

DECEPTION ISLAND - 1964

Telefon
Bay

Chilean Base

Mount
Pond
1778'

PORT FOSTER

Glacier

British Base

Kroner Lake

Argentinean
Base

Whalers
Bay

NEPTUNES
BELLOWS

63° S

Mount Kirkwood
1505'

63° 30' W

0   1   2   **3 Miles**

and coal fumes. On the south side was the kitchen, the most important room on base. Other rooms were the radio shack, the meteorological room, a bunkroom, a bathroom, and a coal-store. The north side of the corridor had two bedrooms, a post office, a darkroom, a library, food storage rooms, workshops, and the second most important room in Biscoe House, the bar. Upstairs were three bunks where the youngest members Charles, Don and I slept. I found out later that we had much more space than other British bases.

Under the hut was a well that stayed at 14° C. Its water level rose and fell with the tides. We didn't have to cut and melt snow blocks like the other five BAS bases. Attached to one corner of the base was the diesel generator shed. Petrol generators were too volatile; in 1948 two Fids at the Hope Bay base had died when their building caught on fire. Outside our base the Union Jack flew from a steel mast; the constant winds shredded the flags.

Like the British Antarctic expeditions of the previous sixty years we used coal to heat our hut. In a chain gang we carried the slow burning Welsh anthracite coal ashore in 100-pound sacks, and dumped them in the coal room, as unusually late summer snow from the northeast swirled around us. Several rooms had small heating stoves complete with coal buckets and pokers. We cooked our meals on a coal-burning Esse kitchen range.

Undisturbed by humans, snow, or the warm beaches, pure white pigeon-sized sheathbills foraged around the base on their web-less feet. I foraged for extra fruit-and-nut chocolate. I was not used to all this exercise after our long voyage, our drinking sessions, and the below-freezing summer tempera-tures. Every Fid helped unload the ship, and would take turns cooking and cleaning up. Scott's hierarchical navy tradition had been replaced by Shackleton's more equitable system.

Apart from the jobs we had signed up for, there were other duties parcelled out. Don, the radio operator, became store man, and was in charge of the library and magazine distri-bution. Charles was the chief meteorologist. Jim Wilson, the diesel mechanic, was the general handyman. Len had meteorology, and was the new base leader. In the position of magistrate and postmaster he was Britain's representative, and both jobs helped any territorial claims. I have no idea how base duties were assigned, but as well as fire-officer, I was in charge of the husky team. Did I ask for the job, or did no one want it? I was pleased, as I had enjoyed looking after dogs at home.

8

Antarctic Huskies

Huskies were first used in the Antarctic on C.E. Borch-grevink's British Expedition of 1899. A few years later Dr. Nordenskjold's Swedish party travelled 380 miles in 33 days with dog sledges along the Larsen Ice Shelf on the east side of the Antarctic Peninsula.

By 1963 the British Antarctic Survey had used huskies for nearly twenty years. The Second World War military *Operation Tabarin* was initially set up at two Antarctic bases, Deception Island, and Port Lockroy further south. The following season, 1944 to 1945, husky dogs from Labrador were brought to the new base of Hope Bay at the tip of the Antarctic Peninsula. More dogs were taken the next season to Stonington Island base in Marguerite Bay, four hundred miles south of Deception Island. Two years later three husky teams from Hope Bay travelled 700 miles in 67 days to Stonington.

In my first year at Deception Island, 1964, the base at Signy Island, in the South Orkneys, no longer had dogs, and the Hope Bay base was closed that year. At Deception and the Argentine Islands, 200 miles south of Deception, dogs were either retired or bred. Young huskies were sent out to the field bases of Stonington Island and Adelaide Island. There, geological and surveying teams used teams of huskies in conjunction with aircraft out in the field.

In the first week of December all the new Fids, together with Mike Godsal the summer vet, John Green, (London BAS office), and the present dog man, John Tait, had a discussion about the Jesters, Deception's husky team. Sandra was pregnant; one of her pups would be kept. Other dogs to be kept were Saki, an old (eight year) white male, two black male brothers, Noodo and Bueno, and Max and his eighteen month old son, Podger, both over 100 pounds in weight. Three females and one male were to be put down. Female huskies were more likely to be culled in order to limit the number of breeding bitches.

Beginning in 1952 each BAS husky was registered. A card gave its birth, parentage, journeys taken, characteristics, and health. Apart from the odd accident, only the best sledge dogs were bred. The males weighed between 90 and 110 pounds, and the females between 60 and 70 pounds. With the year-round feeding, and careful breeding, our huskies were heavier and stronger than their ancestors. However, they still retained a fierce need to fight each other. So each dog was chained, at a non-fighting distance from other dogs, to a thick steel cable, the span, picketed in the ground.

At Deception we fed the ten huskies from the nearby diminishing pile of dead seals. Four-pound lumps of seal meat were given to each dog every second day. In the summer the blubber was removed. The meat at this time was sweet and cloying, and the odour clung to the blubbered stained dog-feeding outfit. That's one reason why no one else wanted the job of handling the dogs. Away from base the huskies would be fed a compact processed meat bar, Nutrican. On returning to base they were again fed seal to regain lost weight. Each dog required two to three seals per year. The seals were primarily Weddells.

The seals, like most Antarctic wildlife were not concerned with humans. I never liked the killing, but the huskies' needs overrode any squeamishness. I would walk up to the seals, and shoot them with a .303. I cut their throat with my sealing knife, and made a long incision to the anus. I was careful not to cut open the lower intestines. The stomach often contained writhing white worms. The innards were pulled out, and dropped in the ocean where cape pigeons would eat to their hearts' content. The seal carcass would be added to the oozing pile of dead seals from the previous year. The killing could have been another reason why other Fids might have been less interested in looking after the Jesters. We were short of seals that season so except for the pregnant Sandra, each dog got two bars of Nutrican instead.

I had my first dog sledge run with John Tait, and two other Fids. Husky handling, dog personalities, existing medical problems, putting on harnesses, attaching said dogs to the traces, and then to the main trace, sledging hints, and learning the local terrain were all started that day.

Later on, when I arrived at the span there would be a steady stream of barking. Most of the huskies would leap around "talking." As I gave each dog some attention the rest would protest; scores would be settled later. Sandra, though antagonistic to other female huskies on the span, also objected to being locked up in the boatshed for her maternal confinement. Every day she chewed her way through 1/2 inch planks to get back to the team.

9

Adjusting to Antarctic Life

Other duties conflicted with my commitment to the dogs. Friday, the 13th of December, was a stressed-filled day. It was my day to cook, and I had my meteorological observations to do every three hours. Because the two De Haviland Otters were waiting for spare parts they had not yet flown south to Adelaide Island. There were eighteen people on base, and meals were in two sittings.

The reception to my first lunch of Scottish herrings in tomato sauce (tinned), mashed potatoes, and carrots (dried) was only fair. The dinner, with a meat mixture, boiled spuds, and tinned peas, fared slightly better. My afternoon Betty buns were appreciated. But I missed the six o'clock met observation in my cooking frenzy, and Sandra escaped yet again. I slept late the next morning.

At the Saturday night bar session the old and new Fids drank and listened to the new records past the sunset at eleven at night and the sunrise at 2:30 in the morning. I stayed up, as I was the early weatherman.

Just as we had solved the Houdini problem by chaining up Sandra, she gave birth to three pups after the prescribed sixty-four days. Then four more appeared. The females were put down, and one of the males died naturally.

The following Friday turned out to be even worse than the 13th had been. Brendan, the base leader, warned me that I had to pull up my socks or else. I was OK in everything except what I was supposed to be down here for: meteorology. I had passed the Stanmore met course so what was the problem?

I hadn't been making careful meteorological observations of the wind speeds, temperatures, dew points, cloud cover, precipitation, etc. After three weeks of immersing myself in Antarctic life I was not focussed on the job that got me there; I was enjoying myself too much. Unlike most British bases, Deception Island intransigents could be sent home up until April. I quietly said I would improve. The warning and day were not forgotten.

The next day, though having had only four hours sleep, my meteorology was better. The vet did post mortems on the four huskies that had been put to sleep. All of them except one had arthritic joints, an occupational hazard of huskies. Under the vet's guidance, I dissected some of Val's abdomen. The male, Steve, had been famous for escaping from Detaille Island base in 1958, when it was closed and evacuated, and then three months later turning up at Horseshoe Island base, sixty miles to the south. In a team he had sledged the route only once before across sea ice and glaciers.

My December troubles seemed to go in threes. We had listened to an inane BBC Antarctic programme with such comments as: "I expect it's cold down there!" and "Don't send any cold to the UK!" The *John Biscoe* arrived, unloaded, and departed quickly. We were down to thirteen Fids. Len, Simon Stanley, the summer microbiologist, and I went on a sledge run. I broke up the first fight while Podger was harnessed up. As usual the rest of the Jesters had turned on him since he was the youngest. In the second fight, as I whomped away at the roaring huskies with a three-inch thick spliced rope thumper, I missed a target. Noodo, unintentionally, chomped on one of my fingers. Podger took off. The rest of the team was brought under control. I was more upset at messing up than being bitten. Brendan put a temporary bandage on my finger.

Christmas Day was not very merry, and it rained. I had difficulty writing my met observations with my left hand. Brendan and Len spent forty-five minutes unsuccessfully trying to freeze my index finger with ethylene dichloride. Years later I learned that this particular medical aid was carcinogenic.

We did have a great feast that afternoon. I enjoyed my first taste of Irish Mist liquor, and my sister's liquor chocolates were appreciated. As usual at Fid gatherings, we voiced our concerns about the British Antarctic Survey. These included BAS promises, the BAS director's vague comments, and the frequent message: "It's all been changed!" We were also short of diesel fuel to run the generators. Fids liked nothing better than to complain. It covered their feelings of having been abandoned even though they were the ones who had signed up.

On Boxing Day, Brendan, Len, Don and I walked the three miles to the Chilean base. There was a mile of unwelcome crevasses on the glacier, but there was a warm welcome at the Chilean base.

Rodolfo, the Chilean nurse, applied two local anaesthetics to my index finger, revived my fainting self, and put in seven stitches. The two-inch scar is still visible today. I was to remain at Pedro Aguirrre Cerda (PAC), for three to four days. The base was named after the president who had put forward Chile's Antarctic claim.

The main Chilean building was much larger than our hut. It was warmer, had better generators, and the Chileans did not use coal. The visiting Chileans and Argentineans always politely mentioned the coolness of our hut when visiting, though they admired our meteorological instruments.

The next few days were busy for the Chileans. A new commander, a summer inspector, and a replacement for Rodolfo, arrived. I kept out of the way. I checked out the records, the two record players, (we had only one), the English books, the air rifles, the football games, the darts, the snooker table, two cats, a small intelligent dog called Timmy, and Aurora, the sister to our base female pet dog, Bertie.

I enjoyed the comidas prepared by Juan the permanent cook. My breakfast of bread and coffee was around 11:30 to 12:00. Lunch, an hour or so later, lasted an hour. I sprinkled the dinnertime with "muy biens," "muy buenos," "si," and "no." Though the officers spoke fluent English, and I tried to learn a minimum of Spanish, I was relieved when Brendan and Len reappeared.

Things went well until New Year's Eve. With a twelve-hour stomach ache I watched a strip tease film, ate chicken, and drank champagne with a stiff upper lip and a grimace. I felt better on the first day of 1964. Charles, Geoff Barrett and Mac McDermott, our aircraft fitters, turned up. With the stitches out and a new dressing I was ready to go. So was the weather.

In gusts of 80 knots the *Shackleton* spent three days running her engines to keep facing into the wind in Port Foster. At the Chilean base, one cast-iron tank shifted, telephone lines went down, and two boats, loaned to the Chileans, were blown three miles across to Telefon Bay. Impatiently I occupied myself shooting an air rifle and playing football games.

Eventually the wind dropped, and five of us set off, sometimes roped, across the now very icy and openly crevassed glacier. The glacier was not the usual icy white colour, but heavily impregnated with black volcanic dirt. Twenty to thirty foot pressure mounds of ice were capped with layers of jet-black ash. It *was* named Black Glacier. Deep inside, the glacial ice water gurgled down to the sea.

I was glad to be back at our base. The Chileans were friendly, but it had been a strain trying to communicate for ten days in an unfamiliar language. When we returned most of the Fids were watching *Dr. No* on the *Shackleton*. I checked on the huskies including Tay, the new pup. Len and I put down Bertie's five unwanted pups. Some chinstrap penguins dropped by our base. The intelligent huskies backed away from the birds as far as their chains would allow; the penguins kept on advancing until it was too late.

Once the planes left for Adelaide Island life was less hectic. I weaned Tay, Sandra's pup. In a letter home, I gave my sister the brotherly suggestion that the assassination of President Kennedy was part of normal, violent, human behaviour.

We tried to clean up the base before Sir Vivian Fuchs, the British Antarctic Survey director, arrived. Summer time was not a clean and pristine time in the Antarctic. As the snow melted, smelly bits of seal like gristle and skin and other forgotten objects surfaced. We grumbled about the visit. Things were back to normal.

10

Some Summer Activities

My weather observations were now acceptable. My other main activity was looking after the Jesters. I would run all of them or just a few at a time. Rain alternated with snow so by February I rotated a wheeled trolley as a "sledge" with an old solid wooden sledge.

At the start of a run the sledge, wheeled or otherwise, was held at the back by a metal stake hammered into the volcanic ash. The main line or trace, some thirty feet long, was stretched out from the front of the sledge and staked. Each lunging husky was placed in its own harness made of lamp wick, and clipped to a short trace that came off the main trace, while the rest of the team roared and barked at each other. Except for the lead dog the huskies were in pairs. The close proximity allowed for fights. When ready the front stake was yanked out, and if things went well the team surged forward. The rear stake was knocked out, and we would glide or bump forward at a steady five to six miles an hour. The beginning of a sledge run was often the time for a team fight.

I learned how to stop the husky brawls with out getting injured. I turned the sledge on its side, thumped the toughest fighters with a thick braided rope to regain my dominance, untangled the traces, righted the sledge, and then set off again. One fight per run was usually satisfying to all concerned.

We would sledge for half a mile along crunchy black level ground towards Kroner Lake, skirt the lake, and head to Lalo Lagoon before the rising rocky moraine of the Black Glacier barred our way. Two or three miles runs were possible. I would run hanging onto the sledge handlebars as we bounced over rough and cavitied black volcanic ash. The wheels of the trolley frequently fell off. On one run Don and I were on, the trolley broke up under us, and the team headed back to base on their own. When there was no snow and no wheels there were no runs.

When we were on snow and came down the steep side of Mt Pond, the sledge rope brake was used. This three inch thick rope brake was attached to the cowcatcher in the front, and dropped under the runners to slow the sledge down. The dogs were generally able to avoid getting run over.

Tay the pup grew longer legged and more confident as he left Sandra to explore the boat shed. He played with Bertie, the base pet dog. Over time he was frightened by a Noodo/Saki fight, comforted an anaesthetised Sandra after her eye was cauterized, stole a penguin from Noodo, and at six months was chained up with the team accompanied by the usual puppy howls.

Bertie, a German shepherd/husky-cross antagonized Sandra, and flirted with both spanned male huskies and Fids. But she came to a mysterious end disappearing after following Len and Charles across the glacier to the Chilean base. She was not seen again at either base; she had probably fallen into a crevasse.

The huskies needed a continual supply of seals. The team consumed one every week, but we only bagged one every ten days. By March our shortage resulted in a quick trip to Baily Head to acquire some chinstrap penguins. Seven seals appeared a week or so later which helped fatten the seal store. One even crawled up to the seal pile.

A summer requirement was restocking the emergency hut with food in case our main hut burned down. In 1946 the first "Base B" hut had caught fire; there were no casualties. (The only British death on Deception was a suicide in 1953). We used a Massey-Ferguson farm tractor to shift emergency food stocks to the nearby Falkland Island Dependencies Aerial Survey Expedition hut, a wooden ex-whaling factory building situated half way between our base hut and the factory. Despite the usual cloudy conditions this aerial survey expedition photographed much of the Antarctic Peninsula from 1955 to 1957 using huge Canso flying boats.

A less strenuous activity for Don and me was shooting at a shop's dummy with a World War One .303 Lee Enfield rifle. We were warned that a ricochet bullet could reach the Argentinean side of Port Foster. Don and Len dug a hole in the black cinder beach, and bathed in the warm volcanic waters as the wind blew.

11

Visitors

In January 1964 our two De Haviland single-prop Otters flew the four hundred miles south to Adelaide Island. With the planes gone there was no Antarctic isolation for us; a steady stream of visitors came and went all summer. With three nations "claiming" Deception's harbour, and with the ease of access for over a third of the year, we had many more visitors than other Antarctic bases. Adelaide Island might get six ship visits a year, and Halley Bay base at the end of the Weddell Sea saw only one or two ships.

"Base B" during the 1963 to 1964 summer season received several repeat visits from *Shackleton*, *John Biscoe*, and HMS *Protector*, the Royal Navy vessel. The American icebreaker, USS *East Wind*, and the Chilean *Piloto Pardo* also called in. Other Chilean and Argentinean vessels moved frequently through Neptunes Bellows. More shipping moved in and out of Port Foster in the summer than through the whole year in Stanley in the Falkland Islands. Seaplanes at the Chilean PAC and the Argentinean Decepcion, bases, as well as American and Chilean helicopters, dropped in on the island.

There would be no films on our base during the winter so we enjoyed the steady diet of films when the British ships arrived in Whalers Bay. The best included *Vertigo*, *The Magnificent Seven*, and *From Here to Eternity*. Most films were not memorable, but everyone enjoyed making rude comments about them.

The visits to Deception Island interrupted my daily routine; it did not feel like lonely Antarctica. I admired Len Mole, our new base leader, for his competent dealings with the steady stream of people. I often got tired of the socializing.

From the middle of January the social rounds began. Len, Charles and two summer geophysicists went for dinner on a Chilean gunboat. Four days later Sir Vivian Fuchs arrived for his base inspection. While I did his meteorological observations, Len followed Sir Vivian around. Apart from kicking the odd seal flipper out of the way things went well. Sir Vivian, however, was not pleased with last year Fids for sawing off two upstairs cross beams to make room for table tennis smashes. Len was rather tired the next day; he had earned his extra 50 pounds in salary.

Two days later USS *East Wind* anchored in Whalers Bay. Len had just finished his night-met observations, but was woken up at 9:30 a.m. as three American Antarctic observers arrived in two orange Bell helicopters. They had "done" the Argentinean and Chilean bases the day before. Being observant Fids we knew who they were as they had the word "OBSERVER" across their backs. A summer geophysicist stalled them while Len got dressed. There were a lot of questions from the observers about the base and its activities. Len was also cook that day so four of us stepped in and prepared lunch.

In the afternoon Captain Henry came ashore to present an *East Wind* plaque, and again Len showed off the base. Some of the crew of the *East Wind* were shipped by landing craft to our black beach to drink their ration of beer; the ship itself was "dry." A large elephant seal also shared the beach, but not the beer. The three Antarctic observers presented us with plastic penguin tiepins. Later we made sarcastic remarks about the natives being given trinkets.

Frequent visitors meant letters got home sooner and more often. One letter from my great aunts only took sixteen days to get to me from the UK. A letter from a friend of mine didn't have my name on so it made the rounds of the bases. I warned my mother that when she retyped my Antarctic letters for relatives she should leave out any derogatory comments. I congratulated my sister for thinking less of the *Rolling Stones* as they went mainstream.

During the social season we adjusted to numerous visits from the Chilean and Argentinean ship and base personnel. We in turn dropped in on the Chilean base, PAC and the Argentinean base, Decepcion. One wet and snowy day while looking for seal, I met a group of Chileans swarming across the glacier from the *Angamos*. At our base Len stepped in as official greeter, and I quickly relearned my limited Spanish. Drinks in the bar postponed our dinner, which was still served earlier than the Chileans were used to. We ended up by having five of them at our meal. They appreciated getting bottles of whisky, and we enjoyed their bottles of wine and guitar playing. And we carried on the Deception Island base tradition. The "Base B" bar tradition was to snip off the ends of visitors' ties and pin then up on our bar wall. Our collection included a snippet from the Duke of Edinburgh.

While the *Biscoe*, further south, was trying to get through the pack ice to "Base T" at Adelaide Island, two British doctors, and Garrick Grikurov, a Russian geologist were dropped off at Deception Island. Garrick geologised, and tried wobli (pronounced wobla), a salted dried fish, on us. It went well with his *Stolichnaya* vodka. Garrick was on a one-year exchange with BAS; the British glaciologist Charles Swithinbank, in turn, spent a year at the Russian Mirny station.

In the middle of February HMS *Protector's* helicopter landed in a cloud of dry dust so that the two Otter air fitters could pick up more airplane parts. The doctors and Garrick were taken south on the *Protector*. On board ship, Len, Charles, and Simon were given drinks but no dinner, though they returned with wine, strawberries, potatoes, and fresh eggs. Again we were roughing it in the Antarctic.

The next day two shiny Chilean Bell helicopters descended on us raising more volcanic dust. A German schoolteacher from Valparaiso stayed for dinner and drinks. Charles and I took him back to the *Piloto Pardo* at the PAC base, in our outboard motor boat; we chugged home in the dark. The day after, Jim and I stayed on base while the rest of the members visited the *Piloto Pardo*. Don returned across the glacier in blowing snow to get the radio schedule out. The others came back the next day accompanied by an American bird watcher.

On one occasion Simon and I walked to the Argentinean refuge hut at Telefon Bay at the north end of Port Foster. On the way back we stopped off for wine and coffee at the Chilean base. Walking back to our base along the narrow beach at low tide we were nervously aware of the glacier's overhanging black and grey ice cliffs rearing above us.

That evening the *Piloto Pardo*, full of commanders and admirals, anchored in front of our base. The officers treated us as equals despite our shabby appearance, though the language advantage was in their favour. Jim Wilson, our diesel mechanic, told of a Fid struggling to speak Spanish to a Chilean naval officer. The Fid was finally asked: "Why don't you speak English, my good man?" Shortly after the naval officers' visit, four PAC air force officers arrived with 36 bottles of wine, apples, lettuce, turnips, coke, and Chilean soft drinks. We briefly thought of those field team Fids, further south, living on freeze dried food and sledging rations. One of our soft drinks, Pico, amused the Chileans. For them "pico" meant piss.

Our permanent personnel doubled in March with the return of the aircrew of Bill Mills and Ted Skinner, the pilots, Geoff and Mac, the air fitters, and John Leigh, the radio operator. The two red Otters had ferried geologists, surveyors, and general assistants with their husky teams for a short season around the Marguerite Bay area and Alexander Island. The planes cruised at 105 knots, took off and landed in short distances, and carried a ton of equipment. They used skis down south, and wheels on the ash runway at Deception Island. An original runway had been built here in 1928 for Sir Hubert Wilkins' first Antarctic flight; he flew south and back for a total of 1,300 miles.

To fly the few hundred miles over sea and ice from Adelaide Island the two planes needed clear weather With the help of the Jesters we established a weather observation camp at the Nipple, 700 feet up overlooking the Bransfield Straits. Then the weather socked in. We returned a few days later, and with the radio, informed the base that all was clear. The two planes turned up four hours later.

The planes "294" and "377" were wintered in a hangar west of the base, and overhauled. I had earlier enjoyed clambering inside the hangar roof helping a summer electrician attach electric conduit.

A few days after the planes arrived Ted took Simon and me on a flight. '294' had a blue triangle with BAS written across it; the symbol resembled the Bass beer logo. We roared along the ash runway, up into the prevailing wind, and circled our horseshoe-shaped island. The rest of the South Shetland Islands rose white from the grey seas. Our cameras clicked steadily. Looking east across the sea we could dimly see the end of the Antarctic Peninsula.

The final *Shackleton* visit brought a new record player, and more importantly, different records, including the *Goon Show*, from the now closed down Hope Bay base. I survived my twenty-first birthday even though it was a day after the Saturday booze up. Jim commented that at this age part of one's anatomy dropped. I ceremoniously cut the birthday cake with a hacksaw.

From several departing Fids I picked up more dog handing tips. On the thirteenth of April there was a wild party of drinking, singing, trumpet playing, horn blowing, and blazing flares for the *Biscoe's* final visit.

12

Deception Wildlife

Most wildlife on Deception Island fled as the winter winds and snows of April set in. The sheathbills and Dominican gulls were the only birds that remained. They lived off the wastes of the dogs and Fids.

While Antarctica has few species they generally breed in large numbers. The inner harbour of Deception Island was an exception. There were no massed birds competing for nesting spaces on the broad sheltered beaches. Life was too risky in the Antarctic to also breed on warm volcanic sand. A few black and white Cape pigeons nested on Cathedral Crags near tiny Wilson petrels. Antarctic terns laid their eggs among the beach rocks, and a few brown scavenging skuas, blue-eyed shags, and gulls nested inside Deception Island. Occasionally gentoo penguins with white triangular head patches and chinstrap penguins with their black chin stripes appeared in our bay.

The seals were just visitors. They pulled themselves up on the geothermal warmed beaches for succour and rest. Some of the crabeaters had one-inch lacerations around their bodies where they had twisted away from the jaws of less successful killer whales. Most of the seals on Deception beaches were the heavier, darker Weddell variety. If they were large enough they became dog food. Fur seals were rare and protected.

The less plentiful leopard seals have spots, and a large head on a serpentine neck. Though half their food is krill they are noted for tossing penguins in the air to de-skin them, and then devouring the bloody carcass. Neophyte Fids have been surprised at the ferocity and large front teeth of these "Weddells with a strange head." I killed one eight-foot male and a twelve-foot female for dog food. The larger female reacted to my approach with opened-fanged-jaws before I shot her. Noodo got the head for food, and I got a three-inch canine tooth as an Antarctic memento.

Below the waters of Port Foster there was more life than on the inner shores. Sea cucumbers, sea urchins, limpets, and purple jellyfish lived in the warmish waters, and after a storm the beaches were sometimes littered with thin yellow brittle stars. The fish were mainly Notothenia, sculpin look-alikes, that had large heads, and, if lacking parasites, were good to eat.

Low tides would occasionally produce pink boiled krill along the warm volcanic beaches. Krill (Euphausia superba), similar to shrimp, are an inch or so long, live up to five years, and thousands of them can be contained in a cubic yard of seawater. They feed on phytoplankton, and Antarctic sea life from whales to penguins feed on them.

Though mostly sterile, Deception Island sheltered in humid spots some thirteen different plants in small colonies. Some were not found anywhere else in the Antarctic. Several mosses and lichens grew there, and Deception had the most extensive mats of the only two flowering Antarctic plants, the Antarctic hair grass and the Antarctic pearl wort. The two plants grew in moss-like clumps, close to the ground.

Along the black beaches lay old bleached whale vertebrae sticking up like forgotten stools topped with green lichen. Inside the bones were minute insects called springtails. These and a wing-less midge were the only true land animals of Antarctica; everything else came from the sea.

Even smaller tardigrades, nematodes and rotifers lived among the plant life.

13

Baily Head Residents

The largest wildlife population on Deception Island was on the outside coast. Baily Head, on the southeast part of the island, had 100,000 pairs of nesting chinstrap penguins. The only inconvenience in getting to Baily Head was dodging the dive-bombing terns along the beach. These small, white, gull-like birds had scissor-shaped wings and tail, a black head cap, and an orange beak. Like the larger brown skuas they were tenacious in defending their nesting areas with diving attacks and ferocious chattering.

To get to Baily Head we slogged through soft sticky snow up a 1,000 feet ridge of Mt Pond. Three times we retreated as cloud covered the ridge. One successful November trip we brought back 250 penguin eggs for our kitchen. A penguin would lay a second egg when the first was gone. To remove the egg I upended the penguin with a gentle boot. It would beak itself in the mud, the egg was lifted, and the penguin re-righted.

On my first February trip with Simon we carried stakes and rescue gear to plot our way through crevasses. In bright sunlight we stood on the ridge edge, and saw the mainland sixty miles to the east; fifteen miles to the north was Livingston Island with its shining white spiked peaks. The Chilean boat *Piloto Pardo* was just entering Neptunes Bellows.

Below us starting as snow and changing lower down to volcanic rock, was an amphitheatre one mile long and half a mile wide. It emptied at a small black beach by the sea. On the right were steep volcanic cliffs that dropped into the sea;

on the left were large open crevasses below the summit of Mt Pond. Covering the whole amphitheatre were multitudes of black and white dots. From below came the harsh cawing sounds of thousands of penguins.

Penguins, possibly Welsh for white (pen) and head (guign), are the southern hemisphere's version of auks. Some fossilized penguins have been found from 35 million years ago, which were much taller than the present day three-foot emperor penguins. The three small Antarctic penguins are the chinstraps, gentoos, and the smaller and more aggressive Adelies. All three are thirty-five inches or less in height, and weigh between ten and nineteen pounds. Each pair shares the rearing of the chick. The chinstraps and Adelies tend to be more concerned with returning to the same nesting site than having the same mate. Gentoos tend to do the opposite.

At Baily Head during the breeding season each one of the thousands of chinstraps penguins would collect rocks for their nests, mate, look after one or two eggs on their nests made of small rocks, and then later regurgitate food into the ravenous chicks' mouths. The more experienced chinstrap penguins nested higher up where it was drier and sunnier. Each nest was a little over half a penguin's length away from its neighbour, and any intruder, penguin or human, was pecked, squawked at, or flapped with flippers.

While thousands of raucous sounds filled the penguin arena, each voice was only interested in his or her mate. Thousands flowed down the hill to feed in the sea sometimes diving to two hundred feet for krill and fish. Seventy feathers per square inch kept the heat in and water out of their bodies. Thousands more chinstraps fought their way back up loaded with food to regurgitate into the chicks' mouths. Each trip was the equivalent of running many pecking gauntlets. Regardless of snow or ash the whole bowl area was covered with white, grey and red excreta shot out at any time and in any direction. As well native green slimy algae covered the ground. The lower one moved down the amphitheatre the louder was the noise, and the more the smell clutched at one's throat. Did Francis Baily, a nineteenth century astronomer, know his name was put to a headland that sheltered thousands of small croaking birds and that reeked of ammonia?

The chinstraps' size of some thirty or so inches did not stop them from attacking the large "penguins" that invaded their territory. But as soon as we passed, the penguins would lose interest. However, the next birds were waiting. We walked steadily through the crowd of protesting penguins, and reached the bottom of the amphitheatre, where incoming waves and penguins crashed onto the black ash beach of the outer coast.

14

Weather

There was no question as to whether one had weather at Deception Island. The question was its frequency and variability. Whatever weather we wanted, or did not want we got; and we often got it on the same day. A short boat trip across Port Foster to Collins Point in fine weather could change to Fids having to seek refuge at the Argentinean base as the wind changed direction and blew with gale force down Mount Pond. The same day could have sun, clear skies, drifting snow, and cold rain. In the summer time low cloud hung like a wet blanket level with the top of Cathedral Crags.

A rapid weather change would have chaotic banner clouds streaming off Mt Pond. The average wind speed at Deception was fifteen knots. A slower weather change showed dark lens-shaped clouds stacked like pancakes over the mountains. Sometimes both cloud and wind streamed through the aptly named Neptunes Bellows.

Although there was over twenty hours of daylight possible on Deception Island the daily sunshine recorder in summer would often show just half-an-hour of sunshine burn. The lack of sun added to the gloom of the dark ash terrain, and affected our moods. Any sunset was a notable event.

Len, Charles, and I alternated with a week of day meteorology, a week of nights, and a week off. In the off-week, daily wind statistics were laboriously entered by hand in the correct columns, and totalled for every month. It was made worse for us in that the previous year's Fids had conveniently forgotten to do their wind stats; I did not hear of any repercussions.

Every three hours the met man would walk between blizzard guide ropes the fifty-yards to the Stevenson screen. As it was near the whalers' cemetery it made night observations a little keener especially if the wind was moaning through the whaling factory. Inside the white-louvered box a barometer measured air pressure, and there were gauges to measure the limited range of temperatures at Deception. An anemometer spun continuously, and gave a wind speed. Each meteorologist observed the sky for the amount of cloud, the type, its approximate height, and its direction of movement. Deception Island weather was cold and damp compared to the mostly cold and dry weather elsewhere in the Antarctic.

The main scientific work done at Deception was meteorology. The observations were sent daily to Stanley for local weather forecasting, and then eventually ended up at the World Meteorological Centre in Melbourne, Australia. The polar areas, especially the larger Antarctica, exchanged cold air and water with the warmer areas of the world. Antarctic weather data collected over several decades has shown a global warming trend.

At the Deception base we would occasionally launch helium filled balloons, and observe their three-dimensional gyrations, and approximate height before they disappeared into cloud or behind the surrounding snow-topped mountains. It was the only task in the Antarctic that I was reluctant to do. I had an irrational fear that the helium canisters might explode.

15

Fids In Winter

The increasing darkness, the worsening weather, and the spreading sea ice isolated us from the outside world. Ships wouldn't drop anchor in Whalers Bay for eight months. Planes from South America might drop supplies, but they couldn't land. The nearest Chilean base in the South Shetlands was fifty miles away across cold rough seas and broken ice. We were on our own. The fact that Deception Island was volcanic did cross our minds. If needed we could have made a one-way trip in the two planes, and ditched them close to a distant base.

More importantly this winter, the Fids had to get on with each other. The question on the British Antarctic Survey job application form as to whether the applicant would be suited to living in confined quarters, would now be tested. We were ten men living in a 1,000 square foot hut. Our world had shrunk.

Our daily routines helped us get through the winter. A typical Deception Island winter's day started with the 6 a.m. weather observation. The night met-man dropped the observation sheets on the radio operator's desk, and went to bed. The rest of the base rose later. Early risers would noisily prepare breakfasts of bacon, eggs (penguin, chicken, or dried), toast, tinned Chivers' marmalade, and tea. The night owls staggered in, looked at the food, sipped tea, and asked about the weather. A keen met-man would reel off temperature, wind stats, cloud cover, and future prognostications. The less keen would give a terse: "manky," (totally cloud covered), or "windy."

Jim, the diesel mechanic, started the generators, and headed in for breakfast with a comment such as: "Number Two Lister is acting funny." He would return later to fix it. We needed electric light and the radio.

Our radio operator moved from the kitchen to the smallest room on base. Once the radio was warmed up, Don contacted the outside world, well at least Stanley. He sent the meteorological observations, other messages were sent or received, and then there would be silence again.

Our personal communications to the outside were limited to 100 words per month, radioed out often in Morse code, and typed up for our families. 200 words were radioed in every month from home. Incoming messages with news of the outside world, though twice as long as ours, often seemed irrelevant. Our communiqués, based on the weather, sighting penguins, and escaped huskies, were more important from our narrow base-bound point of view.

The pilots, Bill and Ted, and the aircraft radio operator, John, were less busy in the winter. Their hectic time was flying the Otters during the long summer days. The aircraft fitters, Big Mac and Little Geoff spent the winter overhauling the two BAS planes. They bickered daily about getting started "now," or "wait a bit." After more palavering they would dress, complain about the weather, and head along the runway to the hangar. Geoff, the chider, rarely got the more placid Mac riled up. A rare retort: "You're a poisoned dwarf!" left Geoff crestfallen.

After a strenuous half-morning of duties, jobs, or recreation, the smoko break arrived. Outside, even late in the morning there would be only dull light. Inside we smoked cigarettes or a pipe, and had tea, bread, cake, biscuits, or hard sledging ration biscuits if there was no bread left, or it had not risen. I had tried cigarettes, but had more success with a pipe. Cigarette and tobacco rations were plentiful. While the cook worried about lunch the rest of us did tasks until one p.m. when we returned for more food.

The gash-hand emptied the toilet, relit the stoves in the morning, and cleaned the kitchen. The coal ash was spread outdoors to join the volcanic ash. The contents of the five-gallon bucket from the toilet, and any other garbage was taken by tractor out to Penfold Point, near Kroner Lake, and dumped. There were no concerns about what the future might think of this "waste removal."

There was full attendance at the afternoon smoko, and also at dinner. The day closed with darning socks, making Antarctic gifts from sealskin, bullshitting, listening to records, and, my favourite, reading. By nine o'clock Don got the rest of the met messages out, the night meteorologist had come on, and the Deception Island day came to an end.

For recreation we often skied. The local rock was too loose for rock climbing, but the smooth inner slopes of Deception Island had the best downhill skiing of any British base. Crevasses were minimal, temperatures were mild, and there was a lot of space to manoeuvre.

I had acquired some skiing expertise on a one-week school ski-holiday in Switzerland. There in the morning we were instructed in ski techniques; in the afternoon we teenagers terrorized the local small boys with our lack of control. They used the well-known f-word to express their displeasure. I wrote up what I had learned about skiing on the way to the Antarctic. I helped several Fids to ski using our wooden skies, and bamboo poles. The fixed bindings and heavy wet snow led to a few twisted knees and ankles.

In mid-May, Don and I ascended Mount Kirkwood's 1,500 feet. A group going to the Argentinean base had dropped us at its foot. I chose a suitable line up the side, and we skirted around large crevasses near the top, and slogged up to the flat summit. Our lightly snow-covered horseshoe shaped island and harbour lay below. Above us high stratus cumulus clouds drifted by. For Don and I the hardest part was waiting in the cold at the bottom of Mt Kirkwood for those who had the boat. They were in no rush to leave the warmth and hospitality of the Argentinean base.

A favourite winter activity was photography. We photographed everything that moved or did not. With just black and white terrain around us, the infrequent colourful sunrises and sunsets were eagerly photographed. We did our own developing and printing of both black and white and coloured film.

Our base photographs of Fids brought out some personality traits. A smiling Len with a balaclava hat and Norwegian sweater relaxed as an Antarctic explorer. He had no Antarctic experience, but his sociability kept base personality clashes to a minimum, and it was helpful with visitors.

John posed as the cool detective. He was casual in his comments, and competent on the radio. He used a sideways knife transmission key to send fast Morse code messages.

Ted's photo has him in a Napoleon like pose on top of a farm tractor. He could see no point in me learning to type by the hunt and peck technique; it was touch-typing or nothing at all. By changing my methods I got up to the dizzy heights of thirty words a minute. Perhaps Ted's abrupt manner was formed by his upbringing: "I was belted as a boy and it did me no harm."

I have a picture of the other pilot, Bill, peering out of his bunk with a smile, and the light reflecting off his baldhead. He had revelled in the "world's best flying club" with the Royal Canadian Air Force. As Bill had to quit after the requisite five years he joined another great flying club, the Royal Air Force. He could compartmentalize things in his mind; when all the drawers were closed he was asleep.

For his photograph Mac modelled as a rather benign beefy bearded Arab complete with dark glasses and headscarf. Earlier in East Africa with the Army Air Corps, he had been a proud member of the Drambuie Club. If you could drink a whole bottle of this sweet liquor you could wear the bottle top in your lapel. He was affable, and perceptive.

The photograph of Geoff, the second aircraft fitter, was as a sardine fisherman complete with sou'wester; his bright eyes peeped out from under the brim. At seventeen he had been on the Indo-Burmese border in the Second World War. His lieutenant firmly told the troops that they could recognize the Japanese, as they were "short, slant-eyed chaps." The first Japanese soldiers they saw were the Imperial Guards, all over six feet tall. Some of Geoff's irritability came from the effects of having lived in a tropical climate; his white blood count caused the Argentinean doctor some concern. At one point in the winter he talcum powered the inside of his sleeping bag; we didn't ask why.

Neither Charles nor I dressed up for photographs; perhaps we were too young and unsure. Once on the base we had little to talk about. My diffidence and sometime carelessness clashed with his preciseness and intenseness. I didn't improve things when I backed a tractor into him at Penfold Point. I now realize his reactions to me defined my personality better than those who were more forgiving.

My photo of Jim radiated a quiet smile though I was not sure whether it was for the book he was reading, or the half-naked pinup at the back of his bunk. He had already spent two years on King George Island, just north of Deception Island, and one year at Stonington Island, further south. Jim had not gone to university like many of the young Fids, but he read widely; he liked A.E.Houseman's "A Shropshire Lad," and he had read Tolkien's *Lord of the Rings* before it became popular.

Jim Wilson was talkative; I can still hear his Border dialect many decades later. He liked to talk about Scotland, and he held my interest with mountaineering stories. Jim mentioned a Scottish Highland winter tragedy where a climber's body had been found, but there was no head. The force of the descent had ripped the head off higher up.

Jim discoursed on social inequalities in Britain at the time. When medical students disturbed the peace a magistrate admonished them, but the young gentlemen were just being high spirited. Those from less privileged backgrounds, but with a similar disturbance were hooligans, and were dealt with severely.

There were no posed pictures of Don, just the later accident pictures. He and I discussed books, and he expanded my knowledge of poetry with Matthew Arnold, ("Dover Beach:" "...where ignorant armies clash by night."), Tennyson ("Ulysses"), John Donne, Yeats, and Don Marquis ("Archy and Mehitabel"). Don had us read Shakespeare's *Richard III* with myself as an unlikely Richard. His efforts to print a newspaper to be read in the toilet was squashed by Len as the first issue contained rather derogatory comments about one of the British Antarctic Survey officials.

I have one photograph of myself in the usual three-coloured patterned BAS-issued Norwegian sweater, a blue rayon scarf that I still have, and an incipient beard. Beards were tried by most Fids. To keep the Antarctic explorer look, some retained them for over two years, others for life. Field people found beards got too iced-up. The picture of me shows a young man with heavy rimmed glasses, and a rather studious expression. At Deception Island I had travelled further physically and emotionally than at any time in my life. Only with hindsight years later did I note the changes, and how I had dealt with others in the small world of an Antarctic base.

On the base I read constantly. My selection ranged from Ian Fleming's *Dr No* to the more literary works of Franz Kafka, Alan Paton's *Cry the Beloved Country*, George Orwell, and William Golding. Reading was my drug of choice. Once as a boy I had been given emergency money for a train trip. Before my mother had left the platform I had bought another one of C.S. Forester's Hornblower sailing adventures, at the Smith's Bookstore. Her comments to me were rather scathing.

Despite my preoccupation with reading I participated in most base activities that winter. I had not had the male camaraderie of military life, nor a father figure to be close to, or to reject, so I learned my male roles as I went along. The older members on the base generally overlooked my faux pas. Our Saturday night drinking sessions helped my social development, and my cooking duties developed my coping skills.

16

Eating...

On Deception Island there were occasional differences with the ten males living together in a small hut. But one thing we all agreed on was the stress of the three days of cooking as each member took his turn. With only ten people on base, and after each one had told his life story several times, there was a limited amount of stimulation. Port Foster and the surrounding hills were interesting, but they didn't change though the weather did. Even the interest in pin-ups decreased with time. As winter drew on, food was our only pleasure with at least five different daily eating occasions. Late in the evening there would be the smell of hot toast and Horlicks to announce yet another stimulating moment.

Whoever was cook needed to make at least one interesting meal each day, and hope that his eight baked loaves would rise, and if successful, would last the three days. The cook was the centre of base attention for those three days. Every meal had comments made about it. Any failures led to flak. My carbonnades a la flamande, despite two hours of braising, still had uncooked flour clinging to bits of the beef. Ted stated flatly he was going to have bread and cheese. I felt dejected. Like every one else, I had a palpable sense of relief when the three days of cooking ended.

Before I headed to Antarctica I had asked my mother to type out some basic cooking steps. She had learned to cook from her own research, and from her mother. Her mother had gone out to British Columbia at the beginning of the twentieth century as a farmer's wife, but knew nothing about cooking.

She had picked up a few hints from the cook at home before she left.

I ate well at home without paying too much attention to how the food was prepared, and my mother was not the most patient of teachers. At Deception Island, with more practice and time spent cooking, I developed some basic culinary skills. One of my reconstituted rhubarb pies had needed more sugar, and my pastries tended to be heavy. But my family's pound cake was always successful. I refrained from voicing my displeasure at other's failed attempts. My turn would arrive soon enough.

Food supplies for the base were dropped off every year. Old stock was rotated. Most of the food was tinned, accelerated freeze dried (a.f.d.), or regularly dried. The slabs of a.f.d. cod looked like pale slices of wood, but with some gussying up tasted reasonable though still a little dry. The a.f.d. meats, potatoes, carrots, and peas tasted better. The cabbage never tasted of anything but reconstituted stalks. On one September trip across the sea ice to Collins Point near Neptunes Bellows four large cases of dried cabbage were left on the ice. No one missed them.

Cheese, butter, marmalade, jam, vegetables, pilchards in tomato sauce, bacon, and some meats were in tins. Only the tinned Brussels sprouts had an off-putting rotten smell to them. The tinned beans "were heard as well as seen." Some Fids didn't like Hunter's Handy Hams and other Hunter tinned meats. I explained that my mother's grandfather was this Hunter. To coin a phrase he had "made a killing" by supplying British World War One troops with tinned meats. His meats also went on the 1953 Everest Expedition. When Mr. Hunter died, his son Ernest retired at the tender age of twenty-four, and never worked another day in his life. Despite this explanation the tinned meats still had limited appeal.

Other food items were a range of condiments, dried drink crystals, coffee, and lots of teas, as we were British. Occasionally Len would drop a nut on a line through a hole in the sea ice. The hungry fish below would grab the nut, and be pulled out. Thin tasty fillets of Notothenia fish would be on the menu. Sometimes the softer parts of young seal were eaten.

Most of us didn't use Gerry Cutland's wild meat recipes from *Fit For a Fid* or *How to Keep a Fat Explorer in Prime Condition*. Gerry had been a cook at the Argentine Islands base, two hundred miles south of us. For brains on toast he said you hit a young seal on the nose, cut its throat, and the brains could then be cooked. Shags (cormorants) needed to be hung for two weeks and blanched. There were many penguin recipes in the book though the birds had a strong fishy flavour. We looked at the recipes, but were not adventurous or hungry enough to try too many.

Our regular meals included risotto, beef Milanese, pork pie, (Jim's), nasigoreng, (Geoff's), and Fid custard. And for the height of sophistication we would have croutons with our soup. We had a steady supply of exotic tinned fruits, such as papayas in rum, plus wine, mutton, and eggs traded from the Chilean and Argentinean bases. The Chileans had live sheep and chickens. Apart from whisky we only had basic staples like sugar for exchanges. Their wines complemented our other bar supplies.

17

... and Drinking

On Saturday mornings every room on the base got scrubbed out. In the evening Len doled out our alcohol and tobacco rations. Since I didn't drink my ration of six cans of beer and used tobacco sparingly, I swapped these for other alcoholic drinks. Each of us had bought additional booze such as wine and whisky from the duty-free ships. With these, plus the weekly ration of beer, and a half a bottle of gin each, we were well provided for.

The bar was the second most important room on base. The bar counter was littered with beer cans, steins, mugs, and darts. Behind, the shelves and walls were crowded with empty souvenir bottles and brand labels of well- and less-well known drinks. The rest of the bar room walls were covered with souvenir flags, plaques, and the snipped ends of visitors' ties. A gramophone, portable and tinny sounding, took pride of place at one end of the room. The coal stove with its mica windows was against another wall. A cuckoo clock's chains dangled above the stove. Queen Elizabeth, in her frame, oversaw the bar's activities from a third wall. Overhead a "modern" acrylic shade framed the light bulbs.

The Saturday night ritual started early for some and later for others. Who ever was night met man had to be reasonably sober for the nine p.m. observations, if not for the rest. The radio operator didn't get there until after the nine o'clock radio schedule. We knew when either Don or John was on the air as our record player picked up the radio transmissions. Our music appreciation was curtailed for a while.

Apart from providing a pleasant break in our routine the Saturday night booze-ups were a time to vent any frustrations against "them," the BAS administration, whether in Port Stanley or London. "They" had to massage our egos, deal with our gripes, and state that things really were for the best. It was better that "they" were the scapegoats than disrupting the unity by having a base victim. The Stanley office was caught between the policies and directives of BAS headquarters in London, and the querulous complaints of base members marooned in the wintry wilderness

On base, personal animosities were rarely expressed even under the influence of a lot of alcohol. A Fid's feelings might briefly surface, but more drinks usually drowned them. There would be no comment on the person's venting the next day.

In the bar the record player was our main source of music. Bill's trumpet and Ted's guitar had a limited appeal; both needed more practice. But we could all sing along with the records. We vocalized along with the *Kingston Trio* when we could, and even when we couldn't. "Hang Down Your Head, Tom Dooley" got better and louder as the night's alcohol flowed. We also helped *Peter, Paul and Mary* in "Where Have All The Flowers Gone," and we certainly improved on the *Limeliters'* folk songs.

I had been to few parties so I had appreciated the musical and drinking education at the Stanmore meteorological school, on the ships, and at Deception Island. I had known about the "number of green bottles on the wall," but my pop and folk music background was limited. I usually preferred classical music. I had once spent five and a half hours at Covent Garden listening to Wagner's "Die Gotterdaemmerung," but it wouldn't have been much use for most of "Base B's" bar entertainment.

However, when I was nicely lubricated, the *Kingston Trio's* mournful Negro folk song "No More Cane On The Brazos" got me going. Mac insisted it was my song. A photograph of me showed a German beer stein I had brought south close by, my eyes were closed, the head was tilted back, and the mouth gaped open; I was obviously past it, but not passed out, and was still singing along.

Religion and politics were either not considered important, or were avoided as topics as they might break the base camaraderie The Saturday night sessions were times for vocalizing. Most Fids at Deception Island had had military training or were in the military; this topic, half in complaint and half in admiration, was a constant: "If it moves salute it, if it doesn't polish it." John would quote the old: "Dear mother, it's a bugger, sell the pig, and buy me out." The British military national service was considered good for males. As Jim often said: "It was a time when men were men and women knew it." Perhaps. Jim also mentioned the young man who consistently went AWOL from national service. The military police would just turn up at his home to collect him.

John related being in Buenos Aires at a time of extreme political protest where the police could do little. The government brought in tough border soldiers to put down the demonstrations.

Mac told of Special Air Service soldiers raiding clandestinely behind the Indonesian borders from British Borneo. Back on base they would claim a bar table by throwing their distinctive blue berets on it. There were never any objections from other soldiers.

Women were talked about, but as an uncertain entity. A young Falkland Islands' girl, who rode a horse bareback whilst making a roll-your-own cigarette with one hand, impressed Jim. He talked about the Montevideo prostitutes working so that they could earn enough money to marry.

Len told us about his girl friend's very good-looking mother. He imagined a scenario where he knocks on the girl friend's door, and asks: "Is your mother in?" I had few female experiences to relate so I listened, put in the odd comment, or nodded.

One night I stayed up until three a.m. listening to Jim tell tales of Scotland. People who live on the border of an ethnic area can often be more enthusiastic about the culture than the inhabitants. Alexander the Great and the Greeks, and Napoleon Bonaparte and the French come to mind. Jim as usual talked as much as he drank. I stayed reasonably sober.

He talked of Scottish climbers like Hamish MacInnes, and characters from the Creagh Dhu climbing club and their climbs. I listened intently through the wreaths of Saturday night's alcohol, and learned more about the world.

18

Argentinean Hospitality

During the year we welcomed the few visitors who came from the Chilean base, Pedro Aguirre Cerda, and the Argentinean base, Decepcion. Our reciprocal visits were three times their numbers. Certainly for the Argentineans it was a nine-mile walk around Port Foster and over the glacier to get to "Base B," our base. The Chileans, though they were closer, made few visits.

The British, however, made a total of at least twenty-seven winter visits either individually or in groups. Two thirds were to PAC, the rest to Decepcion. Were we too familiar, or was it because they had proper cooks and we had amateurs, and we wanted their fresh food and wine? Were the Chileans and Argentineans restricted by military and political policies in their interactions with the British? Was it our lack of ease with the Spanish tongue, or was it that they did not like the cool temperatures in our hut, that made their visits infrequent?

The Chilean air force personnel and the Argentinean navy personnel sometimes complained that a year at Deception Island was purgatory. Many of us had signed on for two years, and considered it a great opportunity.

The South Americans spoke to their families three times a week. Maybe they were not cut off enough. Every couple of weeks we would pop over to PAC, or walk around to Telefon Bay and then on to Fumarole Bay to Decepcion. Around our base footprints and paw prints would radiate in all directions. The Argentinean base would have a few ski tracks, and the Chilean base would have just one or two sets of lonely footprints.

When the Argentineans celebrated the 25th of May, commemorating the first calls for independence from Spain in 1810, most of the British turned up to join in the festivities. We had no national day to celebrate, so we looked forward to a different food and wine break. Two days before the festivities, Jim and I walked over the glacier to the Chilean base. After breakfast we walked on to the Argentinean base in cool weather and at low tide over the ash and snow, and past two very hot steaming beach fumaroles, another indication of Deception's volcanic potential. At Decepcion, Juan Carlos Canape, the CO, greeted us warmly. Like the Chilean base with its nine people, the Argentinean base of fifteen was large and spacious. Jim and I enjoyed a lunch of ravioli and wine. More British and Chileans arrived in the afternoon.

The Fids unintentionally overslept on the day of the celebrations, and we missed the flag raising ceremony. Later that morning I reached the table tennis finals, but was beaten by Carlos Atkinson, another Chilean arrival. Lunch brimmed with both Spanish and English speeches; Len was able to end his with a Spanish quote to a round of applause. More Fids turned up later.

The evening was filled with food, wine and more speeches including a mention of the republic of Great Britain. More wine followed as well as RAF mess tricks frequently involving beer cans. With my long legs wrapped around a chair I did well in 'the pick up the piece of cardboard with your mouth.' We all got slowly inebriated. The Argentineans showed an old British film, *Sanders Of The River* in which the photography was fine, and the outdated colonial views less so.

On this Independence Day there was not a cloud in the sky. More than fifteen miles away Livingston Island's mountains were visible over the edge of Mt Pond. There was a rare vivid sunset, and that night a full moon lit up the white and black of Port Foster as we went to bed late.

We rose slowly the next day, had lunch, and after many thanks, set off for our base in the usual Deception Island wet, windy, and rough weather. We nervously beached the boat near the glacier's snout, and walked the mile back. I fed the dogs, and as cook made a first attempt at pastry.

19

Winter Breaks

On the last day of May Len deliberately slid down an icy patch of snow. Don dutifully followed his leader, and hit some rock. He sustained a cut under his left eye, bruises, a damaged left knee, and with the loss of his right mitt at -10° C, he was cold and in shock. The injured Fid was loaded onto a man-haul sledge, taken back to base, warmed up, and had his wounds dressed. In a photograph taken later a wan unsmiling face looked out of an unfamiliar downstairs bunk.

The next day, with a swollen knee, Don hobbled around on Fid-made crutches, but a week later he obviously needed a doctor's attention. In blowing snow Charles and I launched a red clinker boat, and took Don across the freezing waters of Port Foster to the Argentinean base. Doctor Gonzalez castigated us; Don should have been seen sooner. The doctor injected the knee, straightened the leg, and put it in plaster. With a torn ligament Don needed to stay put for a few days. Back at the base John took over as full time radio operator.

For the next four days a blizzard blew with gusts of up to 70 knots. Inside the base the corridor's temperature dropped below freezing. Outside the temperature slowly went down to -15° C, and icy growlers headed into Whalers Bay. Mac and Charles boated over to the Argentinean base with sugar, as Decepcion's supply was low. Two days of blizzards stopped them from returning by boat. With sea ice forming Mac and Charles walked back to our base for the biggest festival of the year. Don had to remain behind.

The mid-winter celebration of June 21st is the most important day in the Antarctic. Whether it is the mid-point of six months of darkness at the South Pole, or the few hours of dull daylight for us, this day was a turning point. After this date the light at most Antarctic bases got stronger, and the winter, even if it had not yet got to its coldest, would have an end in sight. The mid-winter celebration marked a "we've survived" point. Any mental depression amongst the members came after the darkest time of the year.

Whilst several cooks prepared the mid-winter meal, Stanley sent mid-winter greeting to each base. We decorated our bunkroom, laid the table with a tablecloth, lit candles, and by three o'clock we all sat around the table in our pressed pants, jackets, and ties. Colourful Christmas paper hats were tentatively put on. We gorged on crab cocktails, soup, three kinds of sherry, roast mutton, potatoes, three vegetables, followed by Christmas pudding, nuts, cheese, and a steady supply of wine, whisky, and liquors. We puffed and perused our cigars. The night became wild, wet, and windy both inside and outside "Base B."

The following day began slowly for me at around ten. I felt awful, had a steady headache, and vomited at ten-minute intervals into a bucket kindly placed by my bunk. By late afternoon I felt somewhat better, and dragged myself downstairs. There were the usual cracks about: "You look how I feel," but I noticed a lack of liveliness in other Fids. Having drunk two of my three bottles of German wine, Liebfrauemilch, I would not be giving a repeat performance for some time.

Don still couldn't get back. The thin pancake ice in the bays stopped the boats getting through, and there was not enough snow to sledge around Port Foster. There was no mention of Don's extended stay at the Argentinean base in the British Antarctic Survey's monthly Periodical Reports. Perhaps this was an acknowledgement that some British bases did not have adequate medical coverage. Bill nearly required medical attention. He had walked to the Chilean base, got lost, and fell into a small crevasse. Bill levered himself out from the waist-deep trap, and after three hours of wandering found his way back to our base.

July's diary entries noted a lunch of blue-coloured potatoes, and one day when neither John's nor my alarm clocks went off. The met observations were not sent. Another day we sang "Happy Birthday" over the radio to Andres, the Chilean base commander.

The base water pump and aerial were replaced by four of our more mechanically adept Fids; I was not one of them. However, when the cold-water tap fell into the tank I managed to plug the hole with a cloth and retrieve the tap.

July 18th was a red-letter day; our salaries went from 500 pounds a year to 950 pounds and up. By the end of the month there was a message that the food allowance would be cut by 20 percent as BAS expanded, and the budget tightened.

The winter gloom continued; Mount Pond blocked much of the sun's return. I continued chopping frozen seal meat for the huskies. I was usually soaked by falling wet snow. The nearby snowdrifts kept changing shape with the winds.

The temperature fluctuated between 0° C and -12° C. Hot pokers were pushed up the kitchen waste pipe to thaw it. Eighteen days of gales roared through the month of July. I felt exhilarated by the winds though I slept less as my dog running was curtailed. One blizzard had averaged winds of 65 mph (104 kmh). This was nothing compared to the later winds of 1972 at the French Antarctic base of Dumont d'Urville of198 mph (327 kmh).

As the winds soughed around the deserted Norwegian whaling factory and cemetery next-door, weird feelings were aroused as old galvanized sheets lifted and banged. The wind rose to a shriek before dying, and then rose again. The dead whalers' presence was felt.

On base, negative feelings surfaced as winter wore on. We knew too much about each other, and there was no change. Personal failings were harped on. A couple of Fids trekked to the Chilean base quite frequently to get away from the rest of us. This wasn't possible at most Antarctic bases. The huskies were a sufficient diversion for me so I had less need to visit the other bases. If a base poll had been taken, the same person would've been at the bottom in popularity.

Deception Island's temperature eventually dropped to -24° C. This was the coldest it had been for several years, but it was still considered balmy for most of Antarctica. There was no wind to increase the wind chill factor. And with no wind the base fires burnt less well, and we cooled off inside. Outside the sea froze and then held, even with another storm.

Geoff and I disagreed about the strength of the sea ice. In my great experience of one year, I didn't think we could travel on it. But by the first week of August at -17° C I drove seven dogs including the pup Tay across the sea ice to Decepcion. Geoff and Charles got towed along behind on skis. We wore our full Antarctic regalia; orange, green and yellow parkas, and large brown leather mittens dangled from lamp wick harnesses around out necks. Orange over-pants, and white mukluks kept our legs and feet warm.

Don was relieved to see us. He appreciated Dr. Gonzalez's skill, the cook's gnocchi, and the friendliness of the base personnel. But the endless playing of tango music and the three-hour afternoon siestas got to him.

After lunch the next day we loaded Don, rice, nuts, meat, and tinned tropical fruit juices on the Nansen sledge, and headed home into a cold easterly wind. We veered to the Chilean base for a weather break. Once the wind dropped we returned to our base. Geoff stayed on at PAC.

A day later I travelled on the sea ice back to PAC. I took Geoff and the Chileans some of our goodies, and returned with half a sheep, and more wine, oil and eggs. In poor visibility and drifting head-on snow Sandra led the way back. Like the dogs, I was covered in frozen snow, but I felt for a change that this was the real Antarctic.

The huskies lacked seal meat. The dogs had earlier been fed on tinned corn-beef, brisket, and ham. Now they were reduced to Hunter's steak and kidney pudding, oats, meat powder, and Bovril. Much of it went straight through the dogs. The base dummies (Dominican gulls) and paddies (sheathbills) were also hungry. They gathered at our main door like farm chickens, and scrambled after the garbage as it was emptied into the tide crack in the sea ice.

In August John and Charles, in the old Antarctic tradition of Scott, man-hauled a sledge around the inside of the island for a week. The sea ice was the firmest it had been for several years, but the going was slow on soft snow.

Two days later the frequent cloud gave way to a beautiful clear white day of -10° C before five more days of gales returned. The black ash was hidden, and the snow and sea ice shone under a low northern sun. Four seals were added to our depleted dog food supply. I took the huskies to Neptunes Bellow while Mac and Bill skijored behind the sledge. The Bellows entrance showed open water. Beyond, the Bransfield Strait was packed with broken sea ice.

On the south side of Neptunes Bellows lay the wrecked *Southern Hunter*, a British whale catcher. On New Year's Eve in 1958, the whale catcher, while avoiding an incoming Argentinean ship, veered starboard and landed on a reef. The Argentineans assumed the yelling and waving were part of the year-end celebrations.

We had fifteen gales in August. The changeable weather was why we could not leave Deception Island in the winter. Livingston Island was only fifteen miles away, but the chances of getting solid sea ice, reaching the island, and returning would be minimal even if there had been sufficient light to sledge by.

On one broadcast, Sir Edwin Arrowsmith, the recently retired Governor of the Falkland Islands, spoke to us on "Calling Antarctica." He sounded like a Peter Sellers imitation. Bill's direct family radio message via the BBC had his wife trying to talk to him whilst his two children constantly interrupted with: "Hi, Daddy! Hi, Daddy!" Many of the Fids around the Antarctic Peninsula listened in.

I had already warned my relatives to keep conversations neutral, which they did a few days later for my broadcast. My sister remembered going to BBC's Bush House, being left alone in a recording room, and making bland comments to me. Next my mother carefully explained how to get cakes to rise. You stirred one way only, and stirred from the edge of the bowl inwards with a lifting motion.

Near the end of August I brought Geoff back from the Chilean base. Outside of PAC some Chileans were skijoring behind a motor scooter. Back at our base Don tried skijoring behind the huskies. He fell a few times on the wind carved snow, the sastrugi. A seal looked on from its blowhole, and then disappeared under the ice.

Once while I gutted a seal on the sea ice, Sandra took the team back to the base without me. I pulled the seal a large part of the way home until met by Len, Don and the team.

At the end of August the planes were pulled out of the hangar; winter was at an end. Our cooking schedule returned to one day at a time. The sea ice thinned as the temperature rose. In the middle of September the two Otters flew south to Adelaide Island. We were now five, and felt diminished. But the quiet of winter would soon be broken by the new social season; my first Antarctic winter had sped away.

20

A Dark Spring

The warming spring brought skuas, terns, gentoo penguins, and later chinstrap penguins and Wilson's storm petrels. Charles put rings on incoming birds. The seal pile was no longer depleted. Warm air brought steady soggy snow, wind, and damp dense cloud that sat over Deception Island. The brief brightness of winter was gone. Overcast weather was normal for half the year at Deception Island. On September 20th cloud moved in; the sun was not seen for three weeks. As the season progressed the rainy mist turned to misty rain; we were the 'banana belt' of the Antarctic. I didn't feel that this was the real Antarctic.

And again the social season returned. Jim, Len, and Charles visited the Chilean base on their National Independence Day celebrations on the eighteenth day of September. A few days later I reluctantly traipsed in soft snow with Len around to the Argentinean base. I felt depressed. I wanted the isolation of Antarctica, not a continual round of social visits to prove that the British had as much right to be on this island as the other two countries.

Now it was the birthday of Juan Carlos Canape, the Argentinean CO. There was great excitement especially from Juan Carlos himself, a small fussy man, who wouldn't sit still. We dressed up, and enjoyed roast duck, champagne, and birthday cake. Andre, the Chilean commander, Silvio, the Argentinean second in command, Doctor Gonzales, and Len gave speeches. A salutation followed every speech; I even spoke a few words. When Len, with some help from me, sang Flanders and Swan's

"The Hippopotamus Song," ("Mud, Mud, Glorious Mud!") he brought the house down. There were many photographs, as well as the singing of two tango songs, and the dancing of the malamba. An Italian *Spartacus* film was shown, and Juan Carlos pushed the rudiments of trucco, an Argentinean card game, on us. We were in bed by early morning though some twisted until 6 a.m.

Len and I were up by half past eleven the next day for bread and coffee. For normal meals the first and second commanders and the doctor ate separately from the rest, and were served by a waiter. We also were treated as officers.

During the day we learned from a certain source there would be a greater Argentinean presence in Antarctica. Planes and more naval personnel were to be stationed at Decepcion as well as rockets for scientific purposes. There were also to be more bases opened on the Antarctic Peninsula, and the Argentinean president, some senators, and other political figures were to come down next year for a visit.

The "Malvinas Question," the Argentinean claim to the Falkland Islands, was also discussed. Our source was pro-Argentinean, but was against the current corrupt, military-driven government. All this Len duly sent back to Stanley under the appropriate code.

Whilst at Decepcion we saw one of the Argentinean planes drop supplies from 3,000 feet. There was great excitement when the load landed, and even more when it landed on "our" glacier. We weren't going to get any mail so Len and I looked coolly on.

The Chileans and "Base B" continued to exchange visits. They borrowed some of our paint; like us they were spring-cleaning. The *Shackleton* was already in Stanley. At Deception we hurriedly repaired our jetty for the relief ships as floating ice kept damaging it. We were starting to get on edge.

I hobbled around for the first two weeks of October. I had stepped on a two-inch protruding nail while wearing rubber boots in the wet.

Bill and Geoff arrived from Adelaide Island in a fast three-hour plane flight. '377' needed spare parts. Though for this particular De Haviland Otter the parts would only be good for the next seven weeks. Bill and Geoff's tales made me want to go south. I was given a plane ride around King George Island. The icy and snowy mountains rose from a green ice-free sea. I steadily photographed everything, and got a severe earache as Bill suddenly dropped the plane from 9,000 feet to 4,000 feet.

The next day China exploded its first atomic bomb. For us in our Antarctic isolation what was important was whether the gash man had cleaned up properly, were the stoves lit, and what had the cook for dinner? We were well insulated from the worries of the world.

I did note rather bombastically in my diary that if the hawk, Barry Goldwater, won the American presidential election, I would sign up for another two Antarctic years. We followed Britain's few gold medal successes in the Tokyo Olympic Games.

Melting sea ice and volcanic ash limited the length of the dog runs. Gullies that led on to the glacier always had too much exposed ash for us to sledge any further. As the season advanced the wheeled wagon suffered on the rough ground. With the lack of snow this year it had not been possible to sledge around the island. Only the trips to Baily Head were on snow. My careful copies of sledging equipment lists and dog and man ration tables were put away.

But the huskies still needed regular exercising. One long run had us going behind Ronald's Hill, a lump attached to Mt Pond, up behind a moraine, and then hurtling straight down hill. I crouched low and jammed on the foot brake. The huskies and I enjoyed ourselves.

Like most dogs the huskies had juvenile personalities. They fought, ate, some were allowed to reproduce, and they all needed attention from the "alpha dog" or top member of the team, in this case, me. Tay would crouch, leap, and crow. His voice was not yet deep. Sandra his mother cooed flirtingly until she saw a female Chilean dog named Palustta further down the span, and a stream of bitch abuse would break out. Bueno barked, and shyly stretched when patted. His brother

Noodo darted around barking wildly. Saki the old dog would give a friendly muzzle and croon softly. Large Max would run around the limit of his chain yelping, and then roll on his back. His son Podger just leapt. Palustta would stand on her hind legs.

When sledging Sandra, the leader, generally followed the standard directions of "Auk" right, "Irra" left, "Huit" to go, and "Ahhh" to stop. Our runs, despite distractions such as fights, attacking skuas and terns, wheels falling off, and the occasional desire to just head home, were usually successful. The tougher two brothers, Noodo and Bueno, worked well together. They picked on other dogs rather than each other. Max was relaxed, and didn't pull his over 100-pound weight. On a working team it would have been up to him to pull, or he would have been put down. Podger had weight and youthful energy, but not the killer instinct needed to dominate the team. I enjoyed his laid back personality. Tay's characteristics had not yet shown themselves. With Podger he was to head south later, where conditions were tougher and colder.

Saki, grey around the muzzle, got more arthritic as the winter progressed. Sometimes it was too painful for him to have his harness removed, and he had difficulty in keeping up with the team. When we sledged down hill Saki was taken off the trace, and he limped painfully along behind. It was decided to put him down. Jim offered to do it, but I felt it was my job. One morning in late October I led Saki up to the edge of Neptunes Window overlooking Bransfield Strait. Cathedral Crags loomed up either side of the narrow gap, and a sheer drop fell to the sea below. I fired the .45. Saki whimpered as I grazed him. The next bullet killed him. I removed his wrinkled collar, and pushed him over the edge. I walked back to the base with tears in my eyes.

The following day remained bleak though the weather was fine. My request to spend the next year south at Adelaide Island had been denied. Len was going to Adelaide, Don to Stonington, Charles to Signy to do more biology, and Jim was to head back home. I was to stay. There would be more socializing, more dank cloud-ridden weather, little snow, much ash, and I still would not be in what I considered to be Antarctica.

However, I still had a dog team. I kept busy with my meteorological observations, wrote up the wind statistics, painted the base, indented for supplies for future years, cleared a site for the new plastic hut that was to be built, and did more reading. There was a slender chance I might be able to fly south next September with the aircrew, and with ships in the offing there were letters to be written. The slow insular wintertime had changed to a fast paced spring, and an even faster paced summer time.

21

More Socializing and a Reprieve

At the end of the first week of December, eight months after *John Biscoe* had left, she appeared once more in Whalers Bay. In dull weather we watched the new Fids come ashore. A year ago I had felt overwhelmed at arriving in the Antarctic. I had not been too aware of the feelings of the people who had wintered over at Deception Island. Now I felt what they must have felt. With the *Biscoe's* arrival our cosy world was now open to inspections, questions, comments, and interruptions. What seemed to us to be rough intrusions were our reactions after living in isolation. We wanted to have the isolation broken, but at the same time we resented the disruptions to our world. Winterers in the Antarctic preferred the quietness of winter solitude to the hustle and bustle of summertime. But, earlier announcements of ship arrivals had always got us excited. When the ships veered off to other bases we felt disappointed. We all had these contradictory feelings.

The *Shackleton* came in the next day, and offloaded avgas onto the *Biscoe*. Podger and Tay were loaded on the *Biscoe* to go south, and we had lunch on board. There were howls from the canines, but we enjoyed our meal. That evening the film on the *Shackleton* was mediocre, but we liked having a dinner cooked by someone else. Afterwards in driving wet snow we unloaded the new green plastic hut sections as the black surrounding hills seemed to peer through the summer precipitation. That night I dreamed of clearing slugs off raspberry canes. The outside world had impinged on my subconscious.

Bernie Chappel, Deception's new cook, came ashore. The difference in cooking quality was immediately appreciated. Of equal interest were the new "goodies" that had been delivered. In my case it was crampons, karabiners, my new short MacInnes north-wall ice axe, and more books and magazines. The apples and Christmas present were hoarded.

Our first letters from home after eight months were eagerly read, and replies were quickly sent off. Most of the outside concerns had not changed much, and they seemed alien and remote. I complained about the lack of news in the weekly magazines and the lack of depth in the Sunday newspaper supplements. Our main concerns were still the every day base issues. My sister invited me to have a college friend as a pen pal; I was pleased. My mother was interested in whether the powerful 1964 Alaska earthquake of the previous March had affected us. It had not, although two years earlier a Chilean earthquake had sent tremors along the Scotia Ridge to South Georgia and then on to Deception Island.

We continued to unload, and I continued my reading. I finished the thousand or so pages of *Swanns's Way* and *Within A Budding Grove*, a small part of Marcel Proust's *Remembrance of Things Past*. I enjoyed the expansive and vivid prose.

An old foundation site, suggested by Sir Vivian Fuchs, was cleared for the new plastic hut. We burnt diesel fuel to melt the site's permafrost. On Christmas Day we had a sumptuous meal, but as we were busy, the festival lacked the significance of our mid-winter celebrations.

A steady number of Chilean and Argentinean supply ships came through the Narrows to relieve the base personnel, anxious to get home to their families, and a warmer climate. Chilean visitors descended on our base in two Bell helicopters, and landed in a dust storm. Two Chilean officers, Commanders Poissons and Horn, rolled up to our base in the bucket of our farm tractor. Points of interest for them were the fallen-down whaling station, the whalers' graveyard where Len with my help had put up fresh posts and ropes, and a patch of grass, which had seeded itself from one of the ships and was protected by chicken wire. We had drinks, and photographs were taken. The Fids continued drinking, and were seen later dancing the twist until past midnight.

There was precipitation on a third of the December days on Deception Island; January 1965, had double that number.

More momentous events were taking place four hundred miles south at Adelaide Island. The *Biscoe* delivered more avgas as 80 drums had disappeared under snow during a blizzard the previous year. Bill, bringing avgas in '377,' landed in the uncertain early morning light at the Adelaide aircraft depot, and shut off the engine while the plane was still thirty feet above the snow. The plane crashed, and a landing strut thrust itself up behind the passenger's seat. The two Fids were not injured, though the plane was a write-off. The loss of this Otter meant an even shorter season for the field parties. Distant teams at Fossil Bluff, some two hundred and fifty miles south of Adelaide Island and half way down Alexander Island, had to be brought back immediately. We at Deception Island were only vaguely aware of these problems.

New Year's Eve saw the ship's captain and Jim drinking steadily. The captain was taken back to the *Shackleton* in a less than sober state. Hector, a summer builder, and I followed in our dinghy, and we observed the captain stretched out on the aft-deck. A geophysicist, and the second mate put him to bed. In the dinghy we tried to row back in a thirteen-knot northeast wind, but made little progress until we stopped rowing against each other. We beached near Penfold Point; I waded ashore through numbing water up to my knees.

New Year's Day, 1965, dawned with some sore Fid heads that were not helped by a summer geophysicist setting off a big explosive charge at Penfold Point. He was checking the island's crustal layers.

For myself 1965 began with two weeks that were increasingly interesting, followed by a month of feeling I was in limbo. Pooka, a seven-year old husky who had killed an older dog when young, and Dave Walter, the new base leader were dropped off at Deception Island. Dave had been an S.A.S. soldier in the Yemen area. As a price had been put on his head, he decided to move to a cooler climate.

Sir Cosmo Haskard, the new governor of the Falklands, arrived on British Navy's HMS *Protector*. The *Protector*, a converted net layer, was not ice-strengthened, but did have two helicopters on deck. She assisted the British Antarctic Survey, and showed the British flag in Antarctic waters. The governor came ashore, inspected the base, and had dinner there. Later in the officers' wardroom on board the *Protector* we had drinks, and boiled salmon; all Fids regardless of appearance and occupations were considered officers.

The white summits of Mt Kirkwood and Mt Pond gleamed in the sun as the temperature rose to 10° C. We stripped to the waist, and worked on building new hut foundations. The old foundations were not acceptable to the builders. Our work was interrupted by the arrival of the icebreaker USS *Edisto*. A new American base, Palmer, was to be set up on Anvers Island 200 miles south of us.

Two days later in the usual dull Deception Island weather I received news that I was going south to Adelaide Island for the coming year. I was going to forgo the amenities of Deception Island for the rugged colder south. The cloud kept low for the next few days, but I felt uplifted. Exclamation marks went into my diary and also in my letters home. The British Antarctic Survey tried to accommodate two year Fids; they certainly pleased me on this occasion.

The change meant that Bernie the cook had to be taught meteorology and dog handling. My future career as a teacher must have started here. It was far easier to teach Bernie met work than for us to refine our culinary skills. I for one didn't rag him about his six foot eight inches in height. He was my ticket to the real Antarctic.

Bernie had his first solo dog run: ah, old memories. I demonstrated how to stop husky fights, especially when Bueno *and* Sandra attacked Pooka. There were also the difficulties of keeping penguins from dogs and vice versa. The penguins stood their ground as the huskies bore down on them. And how do you explain to a husky who was just going to pee on a rock that there was a baby tern on the other side?

Len turned over the base leadership to Dave. He took a presentation plaque to the Chilean PAC, and Don wrote the following in Len's honour:

> This day, o dark and inauspicious day,
> E'en though the sun does dare to show his face!
> Unsolders all the bravest band of Fids,
> Whereof this world hold record.
> Great Len! O mighty leader, wisest sage!
> Whose kindly rule thy subjects' hearts did cheer
> Throughout the Antarctic winter's dreadful night,
> Thy minion's loyal thanks do now accept,
> As from the seat of awful majesty
> Thou steppest down to join the common throng.
>
> Yet think not that thy name shall be forgot,
> Or sink into oblivion. Nay! Thy deeds
> Shall echo still when we are turned to dust:
> The graveyard fence and bathroom waste pipe bold
> Will be thy monuments, and testify
> To all th' admiring world thy shining hour.

The poem to Len lasted, but Len's building achievements through no fault of his own did not.

Charles was packed for Signy Island in the South Orkney Islands, 500 miles east of Deception Island. Len, Don and I packed for a colder clime. But for the next four weeks we waited. I helped put up shuttering for the concrete foundations for the new plastic hut, poured cement, photographed base activities using BAS film, met visitors, did my meteorology, discussed books with my mother by letter, and accumulated seal meat for the dogs. But I felt unsettled and impatient. Deception Island had been fine for a year, but now I just wanted to move on. The heavy grey cloud resting on the top of Cathedral Crags matched my subdued state.

Apart from more low cloud and several days of rain, the only major events for the next little while were the February

1965 ascent of Mt Pond in cloud, by Don and me, and the arrival of a Russian fishing research vessel, the *Orochevo*. We were invited aboard the *Orochevo* for a comic film and dinner. The fruit juices and pancakes were not the greatest, but we liked the stew. On the way back, one Fid managed to step into the sea rather than our boat. He was grabbed, and, with his camera, dried out.

A week later at 4 a.m. we set sail for Adelaide Island in the *John Biscoe*. I now had mixed feelings at leaving Deception Island, my home of fourteen months. The next stage was unknown, but in those days of slow boat travel I had time to adjust.

22

Icy Antarctica

Icy mountains, jagged ridges, and cliffs rose from the sea. White fronts of glaciers hung over the sea and dropped ice into the ocean. Passing icebergs and growlers shone under a white cloudy sky as we sailed past more rugged scenery. We navigated through Neumayer Channel, and then reached the breathtaking wonder of the narrow Lemaire Channel with rock faces rearing several thousand feet up on both sides. A few seals observed our photographic frenzy. We reached the Argentine Islands in the evening. I felt I was at last getting close to where I wanted to be.

At "Base F" the following day the weather was cool, calm, and lit by a brilliant sun. Luminous stranded icebergs reflected gleaming whiteness. To the east a few miles away lay the massive white mountains and glaciers of the Antarctic Peninsula.

The Argentine Islands were a small group of rock and ice covered islands no more than two hundred feet high. The British Graham Land Expedition of 1934 to 1937 under John Rymill spent their first winter here. In 1947 the Falkland Islands Dependencies Survey wanted to use the BGLE hut, but it had been swept away by a tidal wave. The first of several more huts was erected. A base had been on the Argentine Islands ever since.

In sunny weather we bumped our way through small pieces of floating ice. We unloaded more coal. I met people I had trained with at Stanmore. There was a higher level of meteorological expertise at the Argentine Islands base than

Kroner Lake and Port Foster, Deception Island.

Volcanic beach steam, Deception Island.

Unloading base supplies.

A typical Deception Island day.

The south end of Adelaide Island.

The downed Otter '377.'

Getting bath water.

Dizzy - not the best husky.

Mike and the Huns.

Some work, others...

Above: The base
at Fossil Bluff,
Alexander Island.

Right. Two king
penguins, South
Georgia.

A young fur seal.

The Polar Star *off Stonington Island, 2005.*

Biscoe House, Deception Island, 2005.

End of Antarctica, leaving Adelaide Island base.

at Deception Island or Adelaide Island. The meteorology involved a radar sonde system for tracking the daily balloon ascents. The balloons carried instruments several miles up, and weather information was sent back on air pressure, wind speed, and temperature. At "Base F" ionosphere research included magnetism and radiation using upper atmospheric measurements. There were fourteen people living on base here on one small island. With poor sea ice and gales in the winter the sense of isolation and interpersonal tensions would have been higher than on the more spacious Deception Island.

The Argentine Islands' base team, the Amazons, had twelve huskies including Max's father, Eddie. A semi-tame skua regularly sat on an outside railing waiting for Hunter's pork sausages. Recently the base personnel had lifted out a De Haviland Beaver aircraft that had sunk in the sea four years ago. On the Antarctic Peninsula mainland the unclimbed Mount Peary, some 6,500 feet high would be climbed by three of the base personnel later in 1965.

We explored the base, talked, and some of us stood on a two-foot high rock in the sea at low tide to photograph the *Shackleton's* arrival. Then the *John Biscoe* headed south to Adelaide Island in changing weather and swelling seas. I felt queasy as we headed to the colder Antarctic.

While we slept that night the *John Biscoe* crossed the Antarctic Circle just north of Adelaide Island. South of 66° 33' the sun did not set below or rise above the horizon in mid-summer and mid-winter.

We anchored off the southern end of Adelaide Island amidst growlers, bergy bits, and large grounded white icebergs. The base huts were perched on a small group of dark rocks. On either side of the base, forty-foot high ice cliffs ran along the coast. Behind the base, a white ice ramp joined a slow rising piedmont glacier, which went north for ninety miles to the end of the island. Rising up from the frozen skyline was the white top of Mt Gaudry, some 8,000 feet high.

Cold air flowed down the glacier and out to the ship. The *Biscoe's* red motorboat, tied alongside the scow, nudged its way through bobbing ice chunks toward the rock jetty.

A chain of Fids passed piles of boxes and heavy sacks from the scow, over the water gap, to a rock ledge. Each of us picked up a load, and staggered up a frozen path. A red Bombardier Muskeg tractor dragged the stores seventy yards along an open rocky space, the 'high street,' to the end hut, Hampton House. Our reward that evening was *Goldfinger*, the latest James Bond film. The cold Antarctic wilderness was a sufficient reward for me.

To the chaos of resupplying the base was the added confusion of redirecting some personnel from Adelaide Island to Stonington Island base, some sixty miles to the southeast. The earlier crash of the Otter '377,' visible on the ice ramp above, had changed Adelaide from a logistics centre of twenty-one Fids to a non-field base of nine.

Far worse, several science and support people had their work abruptly terminated. These Fids were sent home. Some only learned this the day the *Biscoe* arrived; there were many acrimonious discussions. The base leader, John Cunningham resigned, and the BAS field programmes were limited to the north end of Marguerite Bay. A year of poor sea ice was to cause further problems.

Len Mole was now base leader as well as continuing in meteorology. Kenn Back and Roger Owen, here last year, and I were the other met men. Jim Common's job in his second year here was to bring order to the stores. Anything not under cover or piled high would disappear in snowdrifts until next year's summer melt. New Fids were Tom Miller, the cook, George Green, the diesel mechanic, John Noel, the radio operator, and Tom Davies, the doctor.

A brand new Muskeg tractor was carefully floated ashore on the scow, and driven slowly down two planks to a stony beach; with their cameras ready the Fids eagerly expected the worst.

I landed and walked past the red Stephenson Hut where sledging equipment was stored and past Rymill Hut, the radio and aircraft centre. Three of the base huts were named after members of the British Graham Land Expedition of the 1930's. Further on were piles of dead seal covered with a green tarpaulin; the smell of the rotting dog food wafted out from under the tarp. A dump of red diesel barrels added more colour. On nearby rocks were a large number of sledging boxes, human and canine, and several upside down Nansen sledges of little use now, as the base was no longer a field base. On the right hand side of the stony narrow way stood the generator and tractor sheds. Behind them the ice ramp met the rocks of the base. In summer, extra colour was provided at the bottom of the ramp by a band of red algae and, below it, a band of green algae that also survived on top of the snow.

Hampton House was the base sleeping, cooking and washing centre. Directly to the rear of Hampton was a forty-foot rock outcrop on top of which was perched a small red meteorological hut anchored down with six cables. A rope dangled down the rock face for access. Late at night or in blizzards we stayed on top; sleep could be snatched in the hut. Observations were phoned down to Rymill Hut.

For my meteorological observations, I climbed up the rock with the aid of the rope being careful not to trip over the cables at the top for a rapid descent to the rocks below. To the west was the wide Southern Ocean. In the south reared the faint shapes of the mountains on Alexander Island, a hundred miles away. The Russian admiral Bellingshausen first saw the island over a hundred and forty years ago. Ten miles to the east stood the dark Cape Alexandra protruding into Marguerite Bay with the Antarctic Peninsula fifty miles beyond. Like Marguerite Bay, named after his second wife, the cape was named by Dr. Jean-Baptiste Charcot on his 1908 to 1910 Antarctic expedition. North of the base was Back Bay where the odd seal dozed, and then the Fuchs Ice Piedmont that stretched along Adelaide Island. Captain John Biscoe had named Adelaide Island in 1832 after King William IV's wife.

At the coast the ice cliffs leaned over and cracked into the sea. A periodic roar signalled that yet another piece of the glacier had crashed into the summer waters. Inland the piedmont glacier rose to 1,500 feet before meeting the snow covered mountains and heavily crevassed glaciers along the eastern edge of the island. Clustered around the southern part of the island were glistening icebergs that meandered slowly past the base, or got stuck on underwater shoals. The icebergs were fractured, peaked, striated, split, and white with vivid blue and green cracks. Some were the size of automobiles; others were larger than a three-story building. I was apt to forget that most of the iceberg was underneath the sea.

After our one remaining plane headed to Deception Island to winter, the weather stayed mild with wave-clouds stacked over the distant mountains, high winds, and rain. We had been told at the Stanmore meteorological centre that it never rained in the Antarctic. When the glacier got too icy for dogs or the tractors, I ice-climbed with my new short ice axe and crampons on the forty-five degree frozen slope above Back Bay. Later, winds from the south brought swell loaded with brash ice that dumped lumps of ice over the base rocks. Sir Vivian Fuchs, the BAS director, had talked to us on the radio about the possibility of having hovercraft and snowmobiles next year. Three days later at the end of March ninety-knot gusts of wind blew away the Lansing propeller-driven ski machine. In October we found rusty bits of it on Avian Island, a half mile from the base. The Antarctic weather often had the last word.

At the end of the season I telegraphed flowers for my sister's birthday. She was quite chuffed. On a sadder note both my grandfathers had died; I had never met the Canadian one.

April came in with a bang when we moved some heavy metal pup-pen sections, and one six-foot piece tipped sideways onto my head. Roger's shoulder took most of the weight. There was some blood and I received two stitches. I now displayed a finger scar from Deception Island and a small depression on top of my head from Adelaide Island. On the 3rd of April we lit magnesium flares as the *Shackleton* left for the year. The crew responded with rockets. We were on our own.

23

Base Life

A t Adelaide Island base six of us talked until 2 in the morning. The duration of the talking and the inconclusive outcomes said more about the state of our minds than our ability to solve anything; we talked to bolster ourselves against the upcoming winter isolation. The ships should return in nine or ten month's time. The nine of us on base would have to depend on each other; there would be no Argentinean or Chilean winter distractions. For Roger, Kenn, and Jim their base had shrunk from twenty-one people to nine; there would be fewer people to interact with.

We congregated at Hampton House. Meteorologists gravitated forty feet down the rock face to Hampton. John, at Rymill Hut, once the radio schedules were done, headed back up the 'high street.' George worked in the generator and tractor sheds, but always had reasons to go to Hampton House. Most of Jim's stores were close by. Doc Tom's physiological testing took him wherever his victims were. Tom Miller as the cook was at Hampton House. It was our security blanket in an isolated and frozen land.

The stony 'high street' led up to the porched entrance of Hampton House. Inside, on the immediate right, was a cold wooden seat over a five-gallon toilet receptacle. On the left was the bathroom whose hot water tank was heated by the adjoining kitchen stove. Next to the kitchen was the small photographic dark room. To the right were the gramophone and a bookcase full of paperback books, some easy, some classics.

The living room took up the most space. Light coloured walls contrasted with a dark red linoleum floor covered with two red patterned rugs. To the left, hemmed in by a few easy chairs was the coal-fired heating stove with a bent chimney going up through the ceiling. The two small windows that flanked the stove were draped with dark curtains though there were no neighbours to look in. Opposite was a large dining table with its attendant tubular steel chairs. In March we had melted old 78 records, and turned them into flowerpots for our daffodils, that took pride of place in the middle of the table. Behind the table a shelf, filled with paperbacks, ran along the wall. On the end wall hung a clock that observed our goings on; below the clock a door led to our sleeping quarters.

Inside the base bedroom, eighteen wooden bunks were attached to the walls. With only nine bodies there was plenty of choice. I had a middle bunk. I piled books in the back of my three-foot high space. My sleeping bag lay on a mattress, with pyjamas and a pillow scattered at one end. Climbing slings, karabiners, and leather mitts hung down from above. Some people draped curtains across this, their only private space.

George, the diesel mechanic, kept the electricity running. Someone in a previous year had sited the tractor shed in the wrong place, so George, Len, and a couple of others were involved in moving it off its pillar of ice. As a British Army mechanic George had a distant military memory of a missive from above that each man was only allowed one sheet of toilet paper per day. George's explosive retort was: "I use half a roll at a time!"

Doctor Tom Davies's physiological studies involved following his patient of the day around the base. He collected metabolic excretions from urine samples, and took blood pressure readings. This was part of a parallel study in Arctic Spitsbergen on human stress in Polar Regions. Urine and blood pressure readings were taken at set times even if we were rowing the half-mile to nearby Avian Island. Tom's medical degree was from Cambridge. As an "Oxbridge" entrant he differentiated his major scientific studies with a study on Bernard Shaw.

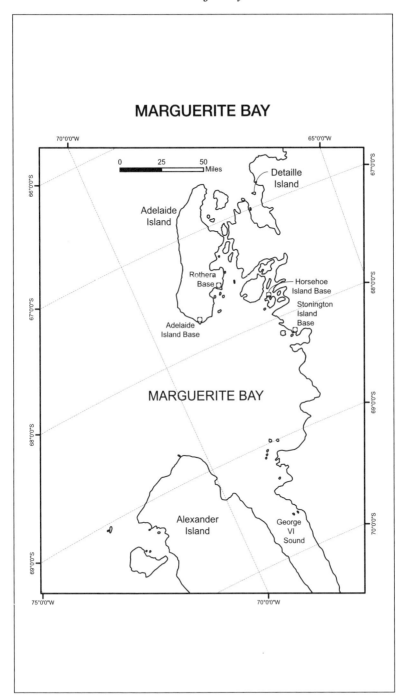

MARGUERITE BAY

Kenn Back with a classics degree from Durham University was quiet and cheerful. As chief met man he kept the paperwork going, and made sure we kept up with the long-winded wind statistics. One balloon ascent initiated by Kenn rose to 67,000 feet.

Roger Owen, another met man, was the prime mover in the base's enthusiasm for developing, printing, and enlarging photographs. I gladly did some of his gash duty in exchange for his developing and printing of my photos. Roger was in charge of the Huns, though I, by doing most of the feeding and exercising, ran them as my team.

Jim Common, with a philosophy degree from Aberdeen, was the tall, relaxed store-man who sorted and stored everything. He once told me that Britain's only contribution to music was the development of the minor third. I took his word for it. Jim recommended Faure's Requiem Mass to me.

John Noel the radio operator was an enthusiastic Fid constrained by the requirements of his job. His outdoor trips were always short. John's comment on my excessive reading was: "Mike, reading is not reality!" I disagreed.

Tom Miller had gone to Gordonstoun School in Scotland where students in short pants rowed boats on the North Sea in winter. He was trained as a cook, and mentioned that there was a lot of competition among the cooks for new and different menus. At Adelaide Island base cooking was less onerous for us; we took turns giving Tom a break on the weekends.

Len in his second year as base leader was keen to help, fix, and do things. His sociability helped dampen most tensions on the base.

For me, Adelaide Island was the real Antarctic, after the damp and dark Deception Island. I cheerfully fed the dogs in blizzards, ran them frequently, did my met duties, and joined in the base activities.

For gash duty, the toilets' contents and the kitchen refuse were pushed down the 'high street' on a sledge to the tidal crack where the sea ice rose and fell. The icy jaws refused nothing though occasionally a pup might be seen strolling back from the jetty with what looked like a frozen sausage in its mouth. Not everything from our toilet made it to the sea. The gulls also benefited from our deposits.

I bathed less often than at Deception Island. At Adelaide, water only flowed off the glacier between mid-February and mid-March. For most of my baths during the year I would push a clean sledge up to a packed snowdrift, and cut large snow blocks with a saw. The blocks were taken to Hampton House, and tipped into the hot water tank. Several hours later after the water heated up I could bathe. As we now had a washing machine my clothes did not have to share my bath.

24

The Huns

When we first arrived at Adelaide Island base in February the mean temperature was 2° C; water poured off the glacier and down the 'high street' to the sea. As on Deception Island rubber boots were an Antarctic requirement. Splashing around the base with the Fids were four pups, named after famous boxers, Sugar, Spice, Ingo, and Floyd.

Silhouetted on the skyline above the base was Adelaide Island's husky team, the Huns. Female huskies were often used as leaders as they were generally more obedient. The Huns, however, had Count, a rather fickle and neurotic male leader

Podger, the new arrival from Deception Island, joined two brothers, Satchmo and Dizzy, (named after jazz players). There was often little connection between the dog names and their personal characteristics. Whatever name was handy and had not been used before, or too often, was the rule. Satchmo, mainly white in colour, would do some work. The weak link in the team was Dizzy who could pull his trace without pulling the sledge. He had a brown shaggy woolly coat that always got iced up in mild snowy conditions. The lumps had to be hammered out. An earlier Fid should have put him down.

Bev, an energetic female, was sometimes deputized as leader. Her only difficulties were breaking trail through deep snow; she was a bit short in the leg. Brownie, another white female, joined the team in March; they instantly hated each other.

The engine of the team, two huskies who could move a half-ton loaded sledge on their own, were the brothers Nero and Caesar. Their drive kept the rest of the Huns moving ahead of them. Unlike most huskies, human attention for them was just a step in the process to go for a sledge run, not an end in it self. Nero and Caesar were the best fighters. They didn't dominate the team as king dogs, but each could trounce any other husky. They rarely fought each other.

Last but not least was the pure white Notus. His left mangled ear was a physical reminder that he had been savaged as a pup. The trauma left him skittish, and vulnerable to more attacks. He became my dog rehabilitation project of the year.

Unfortunately before they could be spanned, two of the pups, Ingo and Spice, died from a virus. Dr. Tom Davies did a post mortem, and found inflammation in their lungs. Floyd got paralysis in his back legs five days after the other two died. Tetracycline saved him.

In the mild weather half of the Huns' pickets pulled out of the ice. The keeners, Nero and Caesar, wandered around the base, followed by the pups. Satchmo just sat at his spot on the span, an indication of his drive. Full diesel drums held the span down until it got colder. The snow around the span was coated with blubber smears, urine, and excrement.

For a short time we had two teams. I made harnesses for the Giants, and drove them. Unlike the Huns who had a tendency to return quickly to base, the Giants kept on running even if there was a lack of scenery as the flat piedmont glacier slowly rose over several miles. At the end of March the Giants were sent to Stonington Island base; we received twenty dead seals in return. Roger and I cut the seals up into thirds before they froze into a solid mass.

Every second day I headed to the seal pile in my greasy seal chopping clothes. I would rip the green tarpaulin away from the sticky frozen corpses. The move was greeted by excited howls and barks from above. With a heavy axe I chopped off four to six pounds of meat, and hooked each hunk into a bloodstained box on a blubbery sledge. Then the husky meals were pushed up the hillside. The intensity of noise and the jumping increased dramatically. The colder the weather the greater was the welcome. As each dog received a piece of meat the volume of noise decreased down to the sounds of satisfied gnawing and chewing.

25

Real Sledging

In the third week of April Tom Davies and I headed twenty-two miles north up the island to Lincoln Nunatak. We were to check on supply depots, the usefulness of a single-side band radio, and Tom was to conduct his blood pressure and urine sampling on me.

I had already started the physiological testing in March. Urine samples were taken every four hours; there was no tea, coffee or fruit juice allowed. I was permanently cuffed so my blood pressure could be taken every twenty minutes over twenty-four hours. My emotional feelings were noted every two hours.

Physical exercise, cold, and emotional feelings were checked to see if they affected the release of adrenaline. My blood pressure was the lowest on base, though it was higher washing dishes than lifting fifty-pound food boxes. The trip's -10° C temperatures and cold winds produced further results for Tom's study. His bottles of urine samples were kept cool stored in a hole hacked out of a hard snow bank.

For the trip I had repaired the lashings on a Nansen sledge. I was finally able to use the Deception Island sledging lists and ration tables. Each human food box was good for twenty-days per person. There were several boxes of Nutrican for the dogs. The heavy boxes were placed on the bottom of the sledge; the lighter radio, sleeping bags, air beds, cooking equipment, spare clothes, crevasse rescue equipment, and the pyramid tent went on top. The reindeer skins and sealskin boots of the past were not used nowadays; Inuit women were not prepared to do the necessary chewing of the skins.

The double-walled tent was pointed into the wind, erected, and checked. The construction of these tents had remained the same in the Antarctic for nearly fifty years. They could withstand most blizzards.

The dogs were harnessed, and weighed. For the weighing they hung from a scale hooked on to a tripod; the dogs became very quiet. Later on audiences became quiet themselves looking at the photographic slides of the "dog-hanging."

Our day of departure had sun, -6° C, little wind, and great visibility. Tom and I were dressed in orange and green anoraks, over-pants, dangling brown leather mitts, white mukluks, and woollen hats. We were as keyed up as the dogs.

Bev, less fickle than Count, was the leader, followed by Count and Dizzy, Podger and Satchmo, then the two keeners, Nero and Caesar, and coming behind, a reluctant Notus.

The first metal picket was knocked out, and as the dogs lunged forward cameras clicked. With the back picket hammered out we surged up to the aircraft depot. Some dogs defecated on the run; to stop would mean getting chomped on by those running behind.

Once we left the tracked area Bev had some difficulty with the monotonous rising terrain, but she persisted up the glacier. Every two hours my urine was sampled, and we had hourly stops for blood pressure and meteorological readings. Tom skijored on skis, pulled along by the team. The dogs and I ran at a steady three miles an hour parallel to the snowy mountains on our right. The Huns produced somewhere in the region of two horsepower. The only sounds were panting, paws and feet crunching on the crisp snow, and the hiss of sledge runners and skis. Despite some soft snow Bev led well. I made one dogleg turn. We arrived close to "No. 5" depot in the evening as the sun slipped below the icy-grey rise ahead, and the light turned dull.

The dogs were spanned out on a thin metal night-wire. The tent was raised, a ground sheet spread inside, and the tent guy lines were made taut. While Tom received the inside gear,

I piled snow blocks and extra boxes on the valance around the tent to keep it anchored. The huskies ate their block of Nutrican, and I put a snow block for water on one side of the sleeve entrance and paraffin on the other side. A radio aerial was run through the ventilation tube at the top of the tent. The dog harnesses were hung up inside the tent to keep them supple, and away from any escapee chewers. I hung my outer gear in the apex, and prepared to relax, unless a dog escaped during the night or the weather did a rapid change. Once fed, the huskies curled up in the snow, and were warm at even low temperatures. The snow drifted over them, and as long as it was not too deep they did not "drown."

Tom started the stove to heat water for tea. We needed a lot of liquids in the dry climate. Dinner was pemmican, potato powder, dried onions, and butter. The next night it would be my turn to make the limited range of food interesting. We tried to contact John at 7:30, but though we heard Stonington talking to a Horseshoe Island party some thirty-five miles east of us we couldn't get through to Adelaide. The final pre-bedtime task for Tom was to pull Nero's rear end into the tent, and add three more stitches to ones he had torn out.

The next day, under a 7/8 alto cumulus cloud cover, we reached "No. 5" depot, a small rock outcrop, and loaded up four boxes of nutty (Nutrican) for Lincoln Nunatak. I managed to tip the sledge twice in an icy wind scoop. Tom, the Huns and I only managed a few miles that day. Bev tended to head towards Mt Gaudry's impressive cliffs and ridges; Notus improved his pulling.

We made another leisurely start the following day, and arrived at Lincoln Nunatak. That day I knocked over one of my urine samples; Tom was not pleased. Our base heard us faintly that evening, but there was nothing two hours later. We slept well despite a night avalanche that roared down Mt Gaudry.

The 25th began with fine weather, and then it quickly manked in. The four nutty boxes were deposited at Lincoln Nunatak. We crossed crevasses to check black lichen on a northwest facing rock wall. The temperature rose to 0° C, and as more cloud came in the snow started falling and the wind came up. The weather forced us to stay put for another day. There was no luck with our radio transmission.

The blood readings stopped, as we were not on the move. I kept on reading *The Brothers Karamazov*, and taking meteorological observations. The only sound outside was snow blowing across snow, the occasional movement of a husky, and the rattle of the night span. Inside we talked spasmodically, and tried variations in the meals; curry helped the taste.

Tuesday saw more low cloud until two in the afternoon. We moved slowly towards "No. 5" depot in deep snow and hard drift. The sledge runners cut, jammed, and protested as the dogs and I panted along in the silence. Sometimes Tom got pulled along. Nero's stitches opened up again, and there was still no radio contact.

Wednesday was another day of low cloud; visibility was only a few hundred yards. My voice recovered from yelling at Bev and to John over the non-transmitting radio. From Tom I learned the difference between psychiatry, psychology, and psychoanalysis. I don't think any were practiced on me.

Thursday was more of the same. Sledging in the temperate Antarctic Peninsula area involved frequent lay-ups in poor weather; not travelling half the time was par for the course. The wind blew all day, and reached force eight to nine (40 to 50 mph) in the early morning. The tent held. We heard later that George, with a Muskeg tractor, was searching for us near the Sloman Glacier, which was nowhere near where we were supposed to be. I finished *The Brothers Karamazov*. The religious and political ideas kept me puzzled and thoughtful.

We got back to "No. 5" depot. Tom searched for lichen, and I took another Nutrican box in case we had another lie up. Even with the thirty-knot katabatic wind that blew down off Mt Liotard, I felt better after my bowel movement that day. Away from base there was always the important decision to be made. Did one face the wind, "moon"it, or compromise by being at right angles? Whatever method, once a hole was made in the snow, one quickly dropped one's layers of clothing, and, watched by the waiting huskies, "chillfully" answered the call of nature.

We headed south. The dogs sensed the Muskeg tracks close to the mountains, and followed them for two hours. The going was tough as we were on a wind-hardened crust with soft sticky snow underneath, so we stopped four miles from our base. We heard neither the Muskeg radio nor the base radio.

The next day we headed one mile too far right; in changing to the left I put my foot in a small crevasse. I hung on, and the sledge pulled me out. At the aircraft depot we met a worried Len and Roger in the second Muskeg searching for the search party and us. At the scheduled hour the two Muskegs connected by radio, and everyone returned. There was much talk; we had not been heard from since the second night. Our radio battery was defective even though everything had been checked. A spare would have helped despite the extra weight. The week's sledge trip even with out radio contact was worth-while.

26

Adelaide Diversions

On our return from the sledging trip, Tom Davies and I practised a crevasse rescue in a nearby large icy chasm. I abseiled in, and photographed the blue ice walls radiating cold; Tom then hauled me out. We should have done this crevasse rescue before the trip.

By May, day-by-day, the light lessened as winter closed in. Smoko became more important. Often the day's tasks didn't start until after the mid-morning break when there was some light. In our isolation we needed the soothing warmth of comfort food. It was getting colder and the nights were getting longer. Cadbury fruit and nut chocolate was much coveted.

Our activities helped keep morale up. Adelaide Island base was a static base. We carried on with past traditions of huddling around a coal fire, and running huskies through the snow. But we didn't need to spend our time preparing for long sledging trips, geologising or surveying in the field, lying up in tents far from base, or writing up field reports. Our jobs were base centred. The rest of the time was our own.

Toboggan racing was one diversion. Roger, Jim, and Kenn challenged John, Tom Davies, and Len. Sledges were built, rebuilt, and modified. Trial runs were made over the next few weeks to develop the perfect toboggan. There was much comment on what was wrong with the other sledge and why this one was so much better. The fastest time down the ramp was thirty miles an hour. I preferred to sledge on my own; my coccyx felt safer. George made a presentation shield for the winner: either the Fated Aces or the Piedmont Pacers. The odds were even. Radios started each run. The racers hurtled down the course, and braked before hitting the rocks below. Roger's group, the Fated Aces, won. Much wine was handed out at Rymill Hut in celebration.

The major diversion throughout any Antarctic stay, second to many Fids' jobs, was photography. Photographs captured the Antarctic; it was proof that we had been to a unique place. The birthday parties, the loose husky or penguin, the brave Fid fighting his way up the 'high street' in a blizzard, etc... All were recorded on black and white photographs or colour slides.

We made up our own British Antarctic Survey Driving Licences whereby one was permitted to drive sledges with up to eighteen dogs plus various mechanized vehicles, and ships of less than 1,600 tons. The licences were stamped and contained our pictures in full Antarctic dress. Scars were noted.

There were frequent sunset shots of yellow, orange, red and purple sky and clouds. There were fewer sunrise shots; though mid-winter produced a few early morning views at 11:30 a.m.

Our mid-winter celebration meal menu was photographed, and we posed for a base photograph on top of the met hut rock forty feet above the base. To quote from Coleridge's *The Rime of the Ancient Mariner*: "We were a ghastly crew." And made even ghastlier when Roger made a composite photograph of us all; it was not any one person from our base. Photos of bowls of cornflakes next to each other became a puzzle for later viewers; or were they a close-up of the ends of cigarettes?

We placed our photographic equipment on the dining room table, and took a picture. There were Nikons, Minoltas, Canons, and one Leica plus close-up and telephoto lenses, attachments, filters, and accessories worth over 1,500 pounds sterling. The equivalent in today's money would be many thousands of pounds.

During the onset of winter we heard that Neil Marsden and John Tait from Stonington Island base had had their tent blown away in a gale. They sheltered in a crevasse, and Neil got a frostbitten hand. His skin shed like a glove, but back on base navy rum helped the circulation. On the radio we listened to the Cassius Clay (Mohammad Ali) and Sonny Liston fight. From where we were it sounded fixed.

The American Antarctic base McMurdo sent a message to all Antarctic bases that one of their men had not returned from an excursion outside a building. There was no chance he would turn up at our base; it was a reminder that a mistake in the Antarctic was costly.

In June over one hundred Adelie penguins invaded the base as a terrific swell sent brash ice crashing on to the rocks. I did my own geological mapping of these rocks. On the radio we heard that two Americans were recovered from a space flight. Six days on, and for us hard to believe, the Beatles received the Order of the British Empire. There was much discussion on the wisdom of this award.

Roger, Tom Miller, and Len shaved their heads though they didn't plunge them into snow banks to check cranial protrusions. I complained of lung pains for several days. Doc Tom's prognosis was: "Just age!"

Despite this cool medical comment I was enjoying the year. I took the huskies for exercise runs past the downed '377' Otter, and headed towards the cold triangular shaped mountains. The snowy wasteland stretched out ahead; after the initial melee there would just be the sound of huskies breathing, and my boots crunching on the hard packed snow. Even on overcast days it was lighter here than on most Deception Island days. On our return as we headed back down to the base the downed plane would reappear, more and more icebergs were seen in the sea, and then we'd be back at the span.

Indoors, I often read a book every two days. A BBC record of James Joyce's *Finnegan's Wake* was too obscure to follow along. I had more success with *Pepys' Diary*, and two World War I epics by Robert Graves and Siegfied Sassoon. Lawrence

Durrell's *Alexandra Quartet* was a warm and lurid contrast to the Antarctic outside.

Apart from looking after the Huns, reading was my main diversion. I wanted to get through as many books as possible. They gave an immediate flavour to my life.

27

Keeping up Morale

The Saturday evening celebrations helped keep up our spirits on our base as well, as on other British Antarctic bases. An added boost was the 160 proof navy rum. This contained approximately 86% alcohol. When gently heated, varying quantities of rum and tinned condensed milk resulted in "moose milk." A Fid's tot, equal to three regular tots, produced quick inebriation. After sampling two of my Fid tots of gin one Sunday John never left Rymill Hut all day.

The custom of BAS drinking came from a male navy tradition, and was another diversion in the frozen environment. We drank on Saturday nights, birthdays, and the arrival and departure of ships. On board ship, officers and crew often drank consistently, but did not, to use a phrase, "go over board." The young Antarctic gentlemen or Fids, on the other hand, did metaphorically. With fewer social distractions from outside, compared to Deception Island, Adelaide Island Fids drank more; our youth also contributed.

As at Deception Island Fids moved into the drinking room on Saturday evenings. At Adelaide Island we moved just three feet from the dining room table. The night-met man decided, based on his condition and the weather, whether he stayed up on the rock, or ventured down. Midnight was a safe time to quit partying. A few colour slides might be shown, but the main accompaniments to the intoxicants were conversation and music.

The talk ranged from holidays to the more important ancillary to sex, marriage. Here, I regretted many years later the lack of written details, in my diary, though by the clear light of a mid-morning winter they probably would have had little importance. We all agreed that if women were in the Antarctic with us they would complicate our lives.

As a topic money had a low priority. We were paid, and most of the money was banked; we had not earned much before heading south. Any philosophical or metaphysical ideas we kept to ourselves. The Antarctic, on a personal level, produced reactions that stayed within one.

Politics was generally of little importance; though I strongly objected to the other's ideas that the immediate democratization of African countries such as Rhodesia would be a good thing since Britain had taken several hundred years to become a democracy. Some of my expressed views went to London via Len's reports. I found out in 1969 on visiting BAS headquarters and Bill Sloman, the personnel officer, that I had been considered to be the resident Maoist at Adelaide. This came as a surprise to me as I had no memory of the subject at Adelaide.

Scatology was of more importance than the above topics. We would facetiously repeat the unfortunate Titus Oates statement on Scott's fatal return journey from the South Pole by saying: "I am just going outside and may be sometime," as we headed to the toilet. Our steady eating meant frequent flatulence, and so were the comments like: "Speak up Brown, you're coming through."

We celebrated four winter birthday parties. The Saturday night was generally quiet before a Sunday birthday party such as Tom D's. His cake went down well, as did the liquor. I noted in my diary that the next day was rather slow in getting going. Jim's Wednesday birthday was another late night/ early morning occasion as was George's Tuesday one. George had a comment about a sergeant who informed his men that the lieutenant would be giving a talk on Keats. The sergeant expected them all to pay attention, as he knew none of them knew what a keat was. Roger's birthday cake baked by cook Tom had a voluptuous maiden draped across it wearing the well-known polka-dot bikini.

As the winter darkness wore on we listened to all the base records and the few tapes we had. The selection ranged from Brahms' *Variations* and Bach's *Mass in B Minor*, (though not for booze-ups), to pop music. We had a recent Rolling Stones record. Years later the facial features of Charlie Watts of the Rolling Stones didn't seemed to have changed much. Bob Dylan and Joan Baez on tape were new and welcome. We appreciated the young lady swinging her hips on Bert Kaempfert's *A Swinging Safari* record cover. "Wimoweh" ("the lion sleeps tonight"), and the South African penny whistle sounds went well with the drinks. We, of course, joined in. Our skiffle group consisted of Tom Davies using a broomstick, a tea chest, and twine for a bass, and John on spoons. We listened to what few Beatles' songs we had. The Beatles had first recorded in Germany with Bert Kaempfert; he fell in popularity as they rose. One of my diary entries compared the female Dusty Springfield's male quality of voice to Gene Pitney's female sound.

The Adelaide base song was "Black Adders." Primarily written by our doctor, it consisted of seven verses pertinent to our year. One verse was:

> The wind was cold and wind blew free,
> But never did we notice any ice on the sea.
> We suffered from the snow and the zero degrees,
> And we nearly died asleep when the bunkroom did freeze.

The tone of the composition can be gained from the repeatable chorus:

> Yo, ho, ho, much mingy woe,
> Damm, blast, and bugger this land of snow.

The complete text may be had on request.

The previous ten weeks of Saturday binges, and a couple of birthdays were a forerunner to the important midwinter festival. The four weeks on either side of midwinter were pitch black save for the dusky light from eleven in the morning until three in the afternoon. The almost complete darkness was restful. The real cold had not started. June's mean temperature was -8° C. The shags, Dominican gulls, giant petrels, and some Adelie penguins still lingered. It snowed every day except one. For us, any personal frictions lay in the future. We enjoyed each other's stories, comments, and quips. Base life was still new after the plane and boats' departures.

On the twenty-first of June 1965 we woke late in the grey morning twilight to tea and brandy in bed. There was more tobogganing, and a Stanley chat programme on the radio. All the Huns were let off the span. We now had three groups. Count cowered at the front door of Hampton House. On being let in he immediately headed for the living room stove, and it was with some difficulty that we turfed him out. The main pack led by Bev roamed the base. The third collection was the oddballs keeping together for mutual protection: Dizzy, Satchmo, and Notus. Once the huskies were back up on the span and fed, we were fed down below.

Jackets, slacks, and ties were worn; I discarded my two-year old Norwegian sweater. Tom Miller, with Len's help, had created a feast with bisque de homard, pate maison, poulet Marengo, petit pois, carottes Vichy, croquettes de pommes de terre followed by an early Christmas pudding, marron glace Antarctique, eau de vie, and café aux Gaels. Other drinks, including my special punch, were added during the evening. Photographs of each person's head surrounded the printed menu. Cartoon body shapes were added for interest. Mine had patched trousers and a perennial book. The music, singsongs, and the skiffle group went long into the polar night. I survived until 5 in the morning. I had learned that one bottle of wine was sufficient for an evening's entertainment.

28

Not a Cold Winter

Two days after the midwinter festivities we had an impromptu rum punch party at 10:30 p.m. that lasted several hours. Some didn't begin the next day until 4 o'clock in the afternoon; work was missed.

Tobogganing carried on as a winter activity, as did skiing on the sastrugi. The temperature rose sixteen degrees from -20° C as cloud moved in. The sea ice stopped forming. The blizzards from the north made it tough to walk in a northerly direction towards Hampton House, but they offered photo-graphic opportunities of us leaning into the driving Antarctic snows, seeing little, and hearing less.

Despite our diminished libidos with a lack of female stimu-lation there was some interest when Nero and the in-heat Bev were put in a pen. Caesar howled all night in protest. He didn't pull as well without his brother.

July's weather finally got to our lowest of -28.5° C, which for most of Antarctica was mild. The month's average was -12° C. The Southern Ocean affected the western side of the Antarctic Peninsula, where we were, so we never had the cold extremes of the rest of Antarctica.

Slowly though, small particles of seawater would freeze, making the sea look greasy. The ice pieces would get larger, and bobbing up and down would become ice pancakes. The pancakes would jostle each other at their edges, and then thicken. New ice below would help dampen the waves. Then if the cold held the sun would shine on a field of flat solid ice.

The previous year, sea ice trips had been made in April. Despite winter storms the sea ice had held, and stayed firm in the inner areas into the summer. This year the sea ice didn't freeze solid until July. Tom Miller first ventured on to the ice skijoring behind Brownie, and the two heavies, Nero and Caesar. Roger and I took eight Huns around Avian Island: "it was for the birds." For the rest of the winter the half-mile trip to Avian Island was all the sea ice travel we managed.

Marguerite Bay's sea ice thickness varied from year to year. The Stonington Island base was reopened in 1958, but closed the following year because of heavy pack ice. In 1961 the new base Adelaide ('T'), and Stonington ('E') were opened. In 1964 heavy sea ice slowed the resupplying of the two bases. *John Biscoe* drifted for over a month in pack ice off Adelaide Island. A forced dumping site was made up against an ice cliff thirty miles north of 'T.' Stores were taken across crevasses, and sledged down to the base. Later the sea ice moved, and the bases were resupplied. Inconsistent sea ice was the only constant.

I had ambitions of dog sledging the thirty-five miles to Horseshoe Island base, closed down five years ago. But gales and mild weather broke up the ice, and I again headed up the Fuchs Ice Piedmont with the dogs. The icebergs off base remained.

Later on in the middle of August the sea ice formed seven inches thick, and was covered with salt crystal flowers. A three-foot high lone Emperor penguin sat on the sea ice outside the base. It was surrounded and photographed. We had seen its belly tracks earlier.

Emperors, the tallest and largest penguins, nested on the Dion Islands, some nine miles southeast of our base. This rookery was, at the time, the furthest north of any Antarctic Emperor site. Though close, the Dion Islands were not a destination for us this year. Sudden gales from the north quickly broke up the frozen pack ice. In May 1958 three men from the Horseshoe Island base sledged west to the Dions. They were not seen again. Nine of their fourteen huskies made their way back to the Horseshoe Island and the Stonington Island area.

The dogs had travelled east for thirty miles over broken sea ice. One of the men, to give the dogs a chance at surviving, had cut their traces.

At Deception Island we had discussions on: "What if the island erupted?" Adelaide Island late night sessions were on what to do if we were on breaking sea ice. Fortunately neither scenario occurred.

On July 18th the sun appeared. It blinked for a minute or two on the distant northern horizon, and was gone. We blinked as well. Over the next weeks the sun gradually stayed longer, and brightened the cold landscape. The few minutes of sunlight made us more aware of the darkness we had been in. We looked forward to more light, and the return of the ship. The sunsets occasionally coloured the sea and the snow on the piedmont glacier with a purple light.

Nacreous wave clouds, iridescent in colour, and made up of ice crystals were observed for two days. These clouds occur ten to fifteen miles up in the atmosphere, and are seen at high latitudes in winter a couple of hours after sunset or before sunrise. Our nacreous clouds had a beautiful mother of pearl shading, and were immediately captured on film. We later laid out a 1,000-yard baseline on the rare solid sea ice to observe other nacreous clouds.

During this winter one of the BAS bases had observed a colourful object in the sky, and it was reported in the newspapers. We were told by BAS to keep an eye out for any reoccurrences. There was great speculation as to what it could be, but there were no further sightings.

When the weather turned colder the base telephone wires wore a coat of rime frost and hummed in the wind. I too would be coated with ice while chopping through the frozen seal carcasses that were stuck together. My clothes, a red headband, green anorak, and brown mitts, added a bit of colour to the white surroundings. The dogs above kept up a steady jumping and yelling. I breathed through my mouth as the nose mucous froze.

Our major warm base diversion for July was building a bar. It was not a necessity, but it gave the base a group project.

Roger was the driving force behind this undertaking. Food boxes in the old hut next to Hampton were moved out. The bar was in one corner complete with a lift-able flap. One irregular bar ceiling contribution of mine did not follow the saying: measure twice and saw once. One tends to remember one's failures more than one's successes. On the last day of July, conveniently a Saturday, Podger officially opened the bar. Everyone except Podger hit the moose milk, and had a late night. We still got on well together as a group. The bar project had helped.

The light in August brightened the sometimes ice covered sea, the white piedmont glacier, and the distant snowy mountains. There was less gloom here than at Deception Island; everything looked white and clean.

One cold night under a full moon, Tom Davies, Kenn, and I walked up to the aircraft depot. Moonlight reflected off the snow, the wide sea, and its incipient ice. The distant Alexander Island mountains protruded above the southern horizon. There was no sound except for gentle breathing and the crunching dry snow.

Another day John and I glissaded down the icy slopes of Back Bay. I got tired of going faster than the toboggans with my skis, so for further thrills I ski jumped. A modest three-foot high ramp provoked some comments, perhaps because I was not tobogganing, but the ski jumps were successful despite the occasional loss of a binding and the odd face plant.

Roger and John carefully built an igloo. It collapsed two days later. John's inability to get away from base because of the radio schedules still bothered him and us. He needed to travel. I sympathized. I wanted more long distance sledging. I tried my hand at learning the Morse code, and manipulating a slide rule, the precursor to the calculator.

George was named base leader for the next year. Once I impetuously sparred with him. Ten days later the middleweight's bruise was still evident on my chest. Doc Tom said I would live.

Unlike John, I could leave the base, but sometimes the dog runs didn't turn out as expected. I gave Count a chance to redeem himself despite hearing of an episode from the previous year when he had taken the team up an iceberg, and peered over the thirty-foot drop on the other side. We had the usual "begin the run" fight, which was quickly sorted out. But Count felt the need for the security of home. He suddenly whipped around, flipped the turned-over sledge upright, and led the Huns back to base. I grabbed the trailing rope hanging from the back of the sledge, and missed. From my prone position I looked at the team heading straight down the glacier towards the ice cliffs beyond Back Bay.

I trudged back to the base to a storm of derisive comments. Worse was my imagining what had happened to the huskies as the rescue was mounted. We skied north along the forty-foot ice cliffs that plunged into the open sea, dotted with broken ice and icebergs.

We found the team. I presume Count saw the base on his left as the team raced down the slope, and he abruptly turned; the team followed. The sledge flipped, and the handlebars wedged themselves into a crevasse six feet from the edge of the ice cliff. The dogs stopped dead rather than being dead. Relieved, we sorted them out, and dragged the huskies to safety with the sledge bouncing along behind.

I got "back into the saddle" the next day by having a short uneventful run, which Count led well enough. I was the "alpha dog," but as was said by many Fid dog handlers, we never had complete command over a husky team. There were too many occasions and dogs to have total control all the time.

We didn't understand why and when the huskies howled. The howling was probably part of the ties that bound the team together, however tenuous the bonding. One dog would start in the evening. Slowly other dogs would join in. The younger one could just yip along. Then suddenly, as if by one command they would all stop.

29

Sledging Further

Fids 'howled' every Saturday night. But despite further diversions such as dart competitions, and making wooden beer mugs and seal leather belts, the month of August started to tell. Unlike those Fids at Stonington Island base we had no spring field trips to prepare for, and the ships would not be here for another five months. It was -20° C, and dark. The old stories had been told too many times. Any tetchiness started now; winter blues was not just a description of cold. I found I needed to get away. The short piedmont dog runs were no longer enough. Stronger sea ice might have helped, but there was none. Tom Miller needed to get away from the kitchen. We decided to travel together up the island for thirty-five miles, close to Mt Bouvier.

Tom wanted more concrete goals so I laid out a grandiose itinerary to get to "Wall," a cliff face below Mt Bouvier. An ascent of Bouvier, some 6,800 feet, was a possibility. I sketched two possible routes. One was quicker and steeper; the other easier except for the initial start. Tom had had some ice climbing practise on the Back Bay slopes.

We set off on a Tuesday at the end of August with ten dogs. Bev, possibly pregnant, was left behind. Count was the leader. The pups, Sugar and Floyd, were along on their first major trip. Once past some rough sastrugi, the four-hour run to Sloman Glacier went well. Subsequent drifting high snow in 30 mph winds made the dogs less keen despite my skiing ahead of them. We camped three miles from "No. 5" depot.

Tom and I had an interesting time trying not to lose the tent in the high cold wind. Extra snow was piled on the valance. Compared to the trip in April, this one was a litany of minor upsets. I had forgotten the steel night trace, so the dogs were harnessed and clipped to the main sledging rope at night. Three of the huskies chewed their traces. We heard John back at the base, but we were not sure if he heard us on the radio. The porridge in the food box was rotten, Tom had to repair a hole in his air mattress, and I damaged my spectacles.

The next day the wind dropped and the temperature rose to 0° C. We reached Lincoln Nunatak in five hours. The Tilley lamp had to be repaired, we broke a spade, and again there was no contact with John. We were only allowed to be without radio contact for seven days.

The third day was a lie-up with high winds and low visibility. Only with a lot of digging did I find my ice axe, and Tom spilt the dinner. We could hear Terry Tallis at the Argentine Islands' base, and *The Archers* radio programme from Stanley, 1,000 miles away, but not Adelaide Island base.

By Friday morning the temperature had dropped twenty degrees C, and visibility had improved. On our right was Mt Mangin at 6,431 feet. Ahead was the Shambles Glacier, and over Mt Bouvier were green and red nacreous clouds. We sledged well for five hours. I ran on the crunchy snow breathing the cold air. When the temperature rose ten degrees I trotted along without my anorak. From our cloth-sledging bag looped over the handles we had access to cameras, snacks, a thermometer, and note pads. We reached Shambles Glacier, two miles from "Wall." Tom was not keen to go any further. We had gone thirty-five miles, certainly better than I had on Deception Island, but I felt like more sledging. The lack of radio communications, the cold, and feeling a bit knackered made Tom reluctant to continue. Count's fight-damaged eye was the final determinant.

On the fifth day we turned back, and travelled twenty-miles to "No. 5" depot in seven hours. Two Smith alarm clocks and a ballpoint pen froze at -25° C. My camera was OK. The radio transmission was not.

On Sunday there was low cloud, and we could only see a distance of four hundred yards. We stayed put, and climbed the lower part of the nunatak. Of course, close to the base the radio worked. Count was injected with 600,000 units of penicillin. Some had frozen, but he got at least half of it, and he enjoyed being in the tent. Tom and I discussed our differences. He didn't see the point of sledging for the sake of sledging. Tom was more interested in the radio. We agreed to differ on both points.

On our final day we got back to the base in three hours. It was hectic putting equipment away, and getting back into a routine, but the base felt like home. Someone had written on my itinerary a few comments on the lack of completion of my trip goals, but if you do anything there will always be those who criticize. My BBC family message came through a day later. There was nothing to cause embarrassment, and I had kept a dialogue going on university options via the regular monthly air letters.

30

Academics, Atmosphere, and Animal Power

M y two-year stay in the Antarctic was coming to an end, and I needed a new goal. I had listened two years ago as most of the budding meteorologists at Stanmore talked about their recently acquired university degrees. I now wanted one.

The British defined people by their educational level. Like seventy-five percent of Borehamwood youth I had not passed my exam to get into the academic grammar school. I went to a secondary modern school where most students quit at fifteen. Some of us stayed for another year to try "O-levels." I took five of these exams and passed four. At the grammar school passing ten "O-level" subjects was more the norm.

For the first time a few of us were allowed to attend the grammar school to try the higher level two-year "A-level" programme. I squeaked by with two "A-levels." Some of the seven-year grammar school students failed all of theirs. My marks, however, were not high enough to enter university.

It was easier to get into most North American universities than to redo my "A-levels." During the Antarctic winter of 1965 I asked my mother to get information from her alma mater, the University of British Columbia, and to collect my academic records. I needed to pass German and physics "O-levels" exams to enter UBC.

Often Fids went to the Antarctic thinking they would learn to play the guitar, speak Spanish, or accomplish some other goal. After two years of slowed-down Antarctic life, most Fids had little to show for the time spent. By my second year I knew what I wanted. I was "under the gun" if I wanted to get into university. My" sit back and observe" attitude at Deception Island was replaced by an academic focus at Adelaide Island. My persistent studying from September to the end of January affected others as well as myself.

I frolicked on Saturday nights as usual, but was less amenable to other diversions. I shut myself off in the bar room away from many of the base activities. My stance exacerbated the need for mutual support in this isolated environment. I kept others at arms length as I studied. There were a few biting comments, and the occasional flicking off of the "study" light. I ignored these, and kept going. I now had a goal in life.

With the Huns, no social overtures were needed. They interacted with everyone. Amongst themselves huskies were the most savage species in Antarctica. They fought from the puppy stage to old age. On runs there was always the initial fight to be got out of the way, and then they would run as a team over the cold flat silence of Adelaide Island. The Huns were more like a regular husky team than the Deception Island Jesters. And the less restricted piedmont gave a feeling of endless sledging.

During the winter, nervous Notus, with firm handling, and as Tom Davies described my "T.L.C.," gradually became a team husky. He could be paired with the laid-back Podger, or the less aggressive females. By September Notus started fights himself rather than being picked on; he would take on Dizzy or Satchmo individually.

During this time George and Jim took off for a three-day trip to test the old Muskeg tractor. The tractor could pull two tons of cargo, and travelled sedately at 4 mph. John with Nero and Caesar rode on the large Maudheim sledge behind the Muskeg, and then skijored back to the base before the wind rose to 80 knots. The next day six of us went out in the new Muskeg to have a party with George and Jim, but did not find them. I enjoyed the ten-mile skijor back behind the tractor as we returned to base, as a lone skier in a white expanse. There was no radio contact with the two travellers.

On the fifth day George and Jim walked four miles in, from east of the base. They had gone off course towards the sea cliffs; the tractor was tilted in a crevasse and stuck. Len led the rescue in the new Muskeg, while John and I followed with the dog team. We sledged down through a mile of crevasses to the Muskeg leaning in its hole. George posed with the tractor for the necessary pictures. The Maudheim sledge was pulled aside, the winch was repaired, and the 'keg winched itself out. John skied back with Nero and Caesar to transmit Kenn's weather observations. Roger and I with the rest of the team led the tractor to safety. Planks from the Nansen sledge were put over open crevasses. Later pro and con comments were banded about over dogs versus machines:

"When the going gets tough rely on dogs!"

"Yeh, but could they pull two tons?"

"Well, when there's crevasses…"

With the arrival of the equinox the weather rapidly changed from cold, bright sunshine reflected off the fresh snow to warm, windy, and cloudy days. One night I climbed up to the met hut. The wind averaged 68 knots with gusts up to 92 knots. Outside I leaned into the wind at a 45-degree angle, and was held up. If I had been blown off the rock my body would not have been found until the next day.

After one night of meteorology, I awoke the next day to find bright new red sleeves and a red collar sewn on to my decidedly tatty and holey shirt. The culprit never confessed.

In the Antarctic night skies shone the Magellanic Clouds and the Southern Cross. They were less distinctive than northern hemisphere constellations. One calm night I saw a meteor fall, as Venus gleamed brightly across the grease ice forming on Marguerite Bay. On the back of a met observation slip I was moved to write:

In the starry clustered dark clear sky,
As ghostly bats (sic) in swooping through the night,
Move through the faces of the stars,
So dips down the riding meteor its light.

Venus' waving light shows the sea,
Reflecting a pillar of rippling gold.
Southerly air moves mildly through,
And the stars flow continually as of old.

For the base a more momentous event at the end of September was the arrival of the aircraft '294' from Deception Island. It was also important for Tony Rider, John Tait, and Jimmy Gardner. With two dog teams these three from Stonington had sledged north to check on the old base at Detaille Island. The base, just east of the north end of Adelaide Island, had been sited on a small island more for the convenience of the ship's captain than access to the mainland. Gales had blown the sea ice out; the three Fids were now four miles from the mainland surrounded by water. They needed human food, dog food, and coal.

The day the Otter '294' was due to leave Deception there was a gale. When the new pilot, Jules Brett, and Mac took off two days later the Otter arrived at the northern end of Adelaide Island in manky weather, turned back, and landed on the Penola Strait by the base at the Argentine Islands. After two more days they arrived, and were greeted by a husky, Sugar, dressed in a skirt. Jules and Mac's arrival at the end of winter livened up our base, but there was not the intrusiveness that there would have been with a ship.

We spent the rest of the day talking, and listening to the Deception Island gossip. Dave Walter and Peter Bird had fallen 400 feet off of Mt Kirkwood, and survived. Peter and Bernie Chappell were coming down to Adelaide next year. Bernie could stop a husky fight by picking up the two rather surprised huskies at the same time.

The next day was a recovery day for most of us, but not for the weather. It clouded in, and then went down to -27° C. A week later with the plane's engine heated up with a Herman-Nelson heater Jules flew the Otter with Mac, Roger and me, the seventy miles to Detaille Island. We headed east, then north up the Laubeuf Fjord, and across to Lallemand Fjord. The island looked rather small, and there was nowhere to land. The three little figures below waved as Roger and Mac pushed supplies out of the side of the plane. The stranded Fids were going to have an even longer winter than the rest of us.

31

Spring, and Flying

October averaged -11° C for the whole month, five degrees colder than September. For entertainment Kenn and I took the "Fated Aces" toboggan over a small ice cliff, and dropped six feet into soft snow; I bailed out before we landed. We also ski-jumped off the same cliff. Kenn and I went on a dog run up the piedmont glacier, bare-chested, to get more tanning rays. The meteorological sunshine card was also well burnt compared with the met cards further north on Deception Island. Earlier at Adelaide I had skied around the base baring my torso in the bright sun; it was another photo opportunity. However, in the shade the temperature dropped below freezing.

Another bare-chested occasion was in the interest of science. I sat in a storage hut for ten minutes at -8° C while my blood pressure was taken. The added stress would presumably show up in my metabolites.

Bev, Dizzy, and Satchmo had a cold experience when they went through the sea ice. Bev scrambled out, but had to go back in the water again as Tom Miller pulled the other two dogs out and then her. I kept Sugar and Floyd out of the hole. The huskies just shook themselves and carried on. Dogs normally put little paw pressure on sea ice. One of many reasons for not using pigs in the Antarctic would be the eighty-pounds per square inch pressure their hooves would make. Other sea ice runs had two dog combinations racing back from Avian Island while Fids tried to sabotage each other's team.

The main thrust of Adelaide's spring activities was supporting the plane's field tasks. After the initial Detaille Island drops, Stonington field teams were given air support. The Otter would carry a whole team and sledge with supplies over a distance of several hundred miles. Only six hundred feet of distance was needed to land if fully loaded, and four hundred feet if unloaded. The weather controlled the plane's flying. The weather, on the east coast of the Antarctic Peninsula where some teams were, could be completely different from the Marguerite Bay side.

The first British base at Stonington had been set in up in 1946 on the island which had previously been used by Admiral Byrd's East Base group. The next year's initial resentment by the private American Finne Ronne expedition when it arrived on the same small island was resolved by combining American aircraft with British dog teams. A surprise for some of the British Fids was that there were two women, Jackie Ronne and Jennie Darlington, on the American expedition. Their gender was not so much an issue as the conflict between their husbands. Later a few of the Stonington Island Fids had a three-year Antarctic sojourn rather than two; in 1949 the relief ship could not get through impenetrable pack ice.

During this October a Stonington husky named Cap, a relative of Noodo and Bueno in Deception Island, was flown in for medical treatment. Tom Davies was taken out to the field to do medical checks on other dogs. One husky with cancer of the mouth was put down. John had one fast trip to Sloman Glacier with the dog team, and next he did a Detaille Island supply drop. I looked after the radio for him while the plane was in the air.

In the third week of October George and Jim were flown the two hundred and fifty miles south to Fossil Bluff, a small base on Alexander Island, to check on supplies. The previous year the Huns had operated from this base. Now seven of the huskies were taken back there in case the plane couldn't relieve George and Jim. Dizzy had flatulence inside the plane, Count started a fight, but everyone survived. The remaining four dogs on base, Bev, Brownie, Sugar, and Floyd, were left to be run and skijored with. I felt a little deprived, and a little less fit, physically and mentally with few dogs to run.

The confinement to the base was getting to me. My cavalier use of Tom Miller's kitchen knives to clean ice from underneath the front door led to a verbal blast from Tom. I restrained myself from retorting that if he cooked more often rather than staying in bed past lunchtime the knives might be put to better use. Unlike at Deception Island the food selection here was limited; having regular meals was important. Talking to the huskies after a long winter was not enough. Tom and my prickly nature were due to clash.

We clashed over another issue a week later. The winter tensions built into the spring; the ship's return was still some way off in time and distance. As at Deception Island, the people I had differences with showed up my personality and theirs more than those who were more tolerant.

Tom Miller later went to Stonington Island base for a break. For most Fids October was remembered for the tragic accident at Halley Bay.

32

Deaths in Antarctica

Antarctic accidents varied from the mundane to the fatal, but the climate, the terrain, the isolation, and the small population resulted in a higher proportion of fatalities than elsewhere. For the mundane we had Don's torn ligament and my dog bite at Deception Island. A few years earlier three sledge teams had moved through a crevassed area on the Antarctic Peninsula. The last dog team and driver fell one hundred and twenty feet down a large crevasse, landed on a snow bridge, and, apart from the loss of two dogs, the only damage was the Fid's bruised thumb.

Serious accidents, however, generally meant death. In October 1963 as we journeyed south to the Antarctic, Halley Bay on the Brunt Ice Shelf at 75° south by the Weddell Sea, had a fatal accident. Two Fids with their husky teams had sledged out onto the sea ice. Drifting snow in a high wind separated them. One team returned to base. The other did not. The search party only found open seawater.

On October 12th 1965, a three-man Halley Bay Muskeg tractor hauling two heavy sledges drove in a supposedly safe area. The dogs were clipped to a steel cable between the sledges. The sledges suddenly stopped. The tractor, ten feet in length, had disappeared down a hundred foot deep crevasse. Ian Ross, the dog driver, could not reach the tractor cab, nor could he make radio contact with other teams. All he could do was to sledge forty-five miles to get help. Eleven days later a relief party got to the crash site. The tractor cab was crushed. The three Fids inside hadn't survived the fall. If the dog team had been in front, despite the drifting snow, it might have spotted the crevasse. But we do not know.

At Adelaide Island we learned of the accident a week later. It gave us pause, and brought home the fact that the shining, sunny Antarctic never stopped being dangerous.

I learned that from 1944 to 1954 there were four Fid deaths, and from 1955 to1965 there were eleven. There was a rapid increase of personnel and bases in the 1950's and 1960's. Over the twenty-two years British Antarctic Survey deaths amounted to approximately two every three years. The causes of death included heart attack, fire, one suicide, drowning, a fall, ulcerative colitis, freezing to death, and four cases each of falling in crevasses and being lost on broken sea ice. Most accidents occurred in dangerous areas. Despite the rapid increase in British activity in the Antarctic there was not yet a safety-training programme.

33

Adelaide Island Events

November, like the beginning of most Antarctic Peninsula summers, displayed low-level cloud, temperatures near zero C, and little change in the weather. The plane was grounded for a month. The three Fids on Detaille Island remained stranded. We were all getting impatient for the first ship to arrive.

The increased light and warmth brought courting, and then nesting birds to Avian Island. Antarctic petrels, pure white snowy petrels, and Wilson's petrels flocked in. More gulls, terns, skuas, and giant petrels arrived. The black-coated shags with their white throats, blue eyes, and orange bills sat on their raised nest mounds.

The Adelie penguins headed down the west coast of Adelaide Island, (swimming up to 20 mph), cut across the island's corner through our base, (generally avoiding the dogs), and, in a steady stream, slid over what sea ice there was to nest among the Avian rocks. We later collected several hundred-penguin eggs, and stored them in flour for the winter. The eggs were edible in well-beaten omelettes, or a cake. When fried the "whites" stayed clear, and the yellow yolk looked like a large penguin eye staring at you, but they made a change from dried egg powder. The skuas kept up their usual routine of snatching any unwatched penguin eggs. We kept the skuas at bay from ourselves by suddenly raising a ski pole as they flew in to attack.

On Avian Island moss was collected for scientific study, and the bright orange lichen and the courting and nesting birds were put on coloured Ektachrome slides. In the interest of science Len tried incubating a penguin egg in a sock nestled in a pineapple can. Later Roger and he made a more sophisticated incubator with a meteorological thermogram to regulate the light bulb's temperature. No baby penguins emerged.

One attempt to get to Avian Island had John and Doc Tom getting no further than fifty yards out as ice floes rapidly moved in and out. Several spectators with cameras watched this floe-hopping and boat-pulling exercise with interest. A later Adelaide Island visitor was a young leopard seal that chased penguins, and played close to our base. And on either side of the base the ice cliffs continued their slow shift into the sea, accompanied by periodic thunderous roars of falling ice.

The leg of Cap, the Stonington Island husky, got better. But he came down with infectious ringworm; red weals poked up from his shaven fur. Cap's bedding was burnt, and he was not allowed to roam. Brownie was considered pregnant. I bet a bottle of whisky that she wasn't. In December Bev came into heat, and by February Bev gave the base some new pups.

Another Stonington Island dog, Coll was operated on for a lump in his groin. Cameras surrounded him in the bar, but he had not received enough pentothal. Coll came to screaming, and I half fainted. Ten days later Coll went under again with enough pentothal to kill a human. A four-inch tumour was removed. This time Jules felt faint. Edwin Thornton, a Stonington general assistant, had to give artificial respiration to Coll, (though not Jules), as he had stopped breathing. Coll and Bev's freedom of the base was curtailed as too many penguins were being killed.

I was unhappy with a BAS plan to ship the Huns to Deception Island and then to Halley Bay. Mac didn't relish flying north twice either. Fortunately the long lasting cloudy conditions led to this plan being scrapped.

The Halley Bay base, first set up in 1956, was to be rebuilt. It was near the coast, and every year saw a large accumulation of snow. Their radio shack was now forty feet below the surface. As the base was sited on an ice shelf, it was the only British base to move its geographical position.

An unusual rumour reached us that a New York tourist company would be visiting the Antarctic for the first time, and charging tourists the outrageous sum of three thousand dollars per person. We were a little sceptical, but got busy making souvenirs of genuine seal leather belts, wooden mugs, etc. No tourists turned up.

A more authentic Antarctic event was George filming with his cine camera ice, snow, huskies in the background, and me pumped up with Dr. Davies' blood pressure equipment. My one hundred and forty-three pound, six-foot frame had not changed over the two years despite the steady eating and drinking. Jules called me "Oxfam" Warr.

After a month's grounding the plane was finally able to take off. The first priority was to supply George and Jim at Fossil Bluff. Mac went on the first five hundred mile round trip. He declined the second trip so I gladly went instead.

Fossil Bluff was half way down Alexander Island by the shelf ice of George VI Sound. In 1821 Admiral Bellingshausen had named the island after the Tsar of Russia. A. Stephenson, W. Fleming, and G. Bertram of the British Graham Land Expedition first sledged this area in 1936. Fossils were found here and further north. This gave more support to earlier evidence that there had been long-term changes in the Antarctic climate.

The flight to 71° south was my furthest trip in the Antarctic. As we gained altitude the base became a mere black speck at the end of our ice-covered island. Below, in Marguerite Bay, a smooth white sheet of sea ice was breaking away from Adelaide Island. To the east the snowy Antarctic Peninsula stretched southwards. We droned on towards the white mountains and glaciers of the peninsula, Alexander Island, and the frozen twenty-mile wide George VI Sound; I took pictures non-stop. The plane few past mountainous striated ridges, white on the south side and black on the north. Shining icy glaciers cut by hundreds of crevasses poured through the mountains into the sound. In the distance, unknown pyramidal peaks stuck up through the ice fields of the island. Alexander Island spread south for two hundred and fifty miles and was over a hundred miles wide.

The Fossil Bluff hut stood on a small ridge above the silent sound, looking tiny below the sedimentary layers of the high bluff above. Six Nansen sledges covered the roof. A red Muskeg tractor rested nearby, and below, on a span, were the Huns. I renewed my acquaintance with the Huns, and with Jim and George, who stood outside the hut in plaid shirts looking like gold miners in the Yukon.

Below us the white sound ran for over a hundred miles north and south of Fossil Bluff. Twenty-miles to the east across the sound, the Battterbee Mountains and more glaciers were the only definitive scenery. Behind was the six thousand foot high empty snow plateau, stretching even further to the main Antarctic continent.

With the long throbbing plane noises still drumming in my ears, I later took another plane trip from Adelaide to Stonington with John, Cap, some music records, and a few penguin eggs. Unusual for a husky, Cap howled all the way. John did a switch at Stonington with Don, who came back with Tom Miller and us. Don and I talked steadily back and forth about our local news, and compared books we had read.

We dropped in on Blind Bay, a flat ice-bound bay dotted with frozen-in icebergs, and surrounded by dark cliffs and precipitous ridges. Two young bitches were delivered to Dave Mathew, a geologist, and Jim Steen, a general assistant.

With Mac's continual maintenance of the plane, Jules and Mac were able to take off next for the Larsen Ice Shelf on the east coast. They were back by 2 a.m. I helped anchor the Otter, and was in bed by 3:30.

Now the dog runs were done late at night when the surface froze a little after the sun's melting of the snow. As we neared the summer solstice the midnight sun shone from the south over the distant mountains of Alexander Island for a rare picture moment.

At this time there was continuous daylight, which made sleep difficult. We were all getting restless waiting for the arrival of the first boat. By the first week of December Tom M. went to bed by 10 a.m. and awoke at 5 p.m. This did not bother me so much as his shooting of skuas. I talked to him about this. A few days later we had skua for dinner.

Christmas had fresh snow, and Kenn put up some decorations. We had an enormous meal, lots of drinks, followed by the usual lethargy. New Year's Eve meant more Bell's Whisky, and the New Year of 1966 brought rain, sleet, and mist. Water started flowing off the glacier.

The only possible reaction to our restlessness and routine were trips away from the base. Neil Marsden, a surveyor from Stonington Island, Roger, and I laid a line of diesel drums towards the mountains to aid returning trippers. According to those in the Otter the last marker drum near the mountains was sitting on a huge crevasse three times the width of the Muskeg tractor. I had driven across the snow-hidden hole twice.

When George and Jim returned with the Huns from Fossil Bluff I drove the dogs quickly down to the span. I just avoided some projecting avgas drums in my excitement. A day or so later out on the glacier Kenn and I removed the crevasse-sitting drum. We couldn't see anything, but we didn't linger.

Several other trips up the island were taken. On one trip Notus pulled well, and then he bit Podger. Count's misbehaviour led to the dropping of a vowel in his name. Stanley inquired why so many Fids were off base. A hurried response was made as to the importance of these trips.

At Detaille Island John Tait boated Tony Rider, twelve huskies, food, and a sledge to Johnstone's Point on the mainland. John returned to Detaille through difficult sea ice. The idea was to forge a way up icefalls to an area where the plane could pick the Fids up, or they could sledge back. The movement of sea ice stopped further boat trips; the stranded party was now split in two. A London missive stressed that these Fids were to stay put, and Jules was not to take any risks with the plane though one beer was dropped to a stranded Tony.

By the end of December ships were on their way to Marguerite Bay. Field teams and trippers started making their way back to base. At Lincoln Nunatak Edwin played chess by radio with Jimmy Gardner at Detaille Island, but the three marooned Fids were not going to leave their tiny island.

On January 8th I loaded supplies, a sledge, and most of the Huns into the Otter for my last Antarctic sledging trip. I was flown up to Neil and Edwin's encampment near Mt Mangin. Neil surveyed in bright sun, and I ended up with a sunburned face from the extreme glare. We regrouped a few miles north of Lincoln Nunatak. I was in my element. Then the clouds rolled in, and we had a sustained lie-up.

Edwin and I played chess, we heard about Kenn "Bacchus" boozing it up at Stonington, and we listened to the date of *John Biscoe's* arrival at Adelaide: 20th of January. Now the teams, some as far off as a hundred miles, raced for Stonington Island base. We sat in cloud whilst Edwin kept beating me at chess, and I consoled myself with a bottle of Sauterne. We talked of life. Edwin could see little point to it; it was interesting for me to argue a non-cynical view of life. John had always accused me of being the base cynic.

The mank rolled down from the Shambles Glacier for six days. Edwin decided to move, though Neil was less keen. In a one hundred yard visibility Edwin used a compass bearing and a dogleg turn to get us to Lincoln Nunatak. My job was to keep the Huns from overrunning Edwin's team, the Moomins. Neil and I discussed a particular stroppy Stonington Fid. As we neared "No. 5" depot, the cloud lifted though Neil couldn't see the coloured edges of the cloud. He said he was colour-blind. I photographed the team's shadow and mine trotting along in the early morning sunshine on crisp white snow. We turned up at the base on the 15th after having been up for thirty hours. Breakfast, gash duty, and sleep from 3 p.m. for six hours were followed by more sleep, early in the morning. The end of my Antarctica stay was near.

34

Base Life Comes to a Stop

I felt tired after six days of staying in a tent though my blood pressure back on base showed a high level of fitness. Like most Fids I was unsettled. The *John Biscoe* was due at any time. I was leery of change, and having to leave my current home. But it was time to move on, and deal with a new phase of my life. My diary entries became short. I noted Fid's interest in women's magazines, especially on how to keep a man happy, the various letters of complaint from women in the magazines, and the often hard-edged replies. We were mentally preparing for a not too distant change. But there was still the question, "Why do I have to leave now?" There was never an easy way to leave the Antarctic. My comfortable, isolated existence with lots to eat, drink and read was to be left behind.

The *Biscoe* arrived at nine in the morning on the twentieth of January. For once every one was up. Len went aboard to speak with the Governor of the Falkland Islands. Only summer jetty builders, including Jim Wilson, were dropped off. Peter Bird from Deception Island, and Dennis Horley dropped in to have a look. Dennis had been a year behind me at Borehamwood Grammar School, and was destined to be a general assistant at Stonington Island base. Seeing Dennis reinforced my wish to stay on.

We received a large quantity of mail. I had the satirical *Private Eye*, *Time* magazine, and the University of British Columbia calendar on which I spent a whole day working out university courses. I wrote a twelve-page double-sided letter home.

For Len and Tom Miller there were "Dear John's." It would be understandable for Tom to receive one after being away for a whole year, but how could Len's girl have put her life on hold for almost two years? She had obviously thought he had been worth waiting for. There was another big imbibing session to compensate.

The Governor, Sir Cosmo Haskard, was flown to Stonington Island base, and two days later arrived back to stay the night with us. The Governor's Avian Island trip with Len and Tom Davies was interrupted as the explosives expert, Ken Doyle, had his skull cracked open by standing too close to falling rock while demolishing rocks at the jetty. Roger and I set off in a leaky red boat to get Doc Davies. The engine stopped every fifty-yards. I rowed and bailed as needed. Having got Tom back to base to put six stitches in Ken's head, I returned to Avian Island to tow the Governor, Len, and Roger back.

The Governor's presence seemed to unsettle us. I stepped into the sea over my gumboots, and tipped a plate over myself at dinner. Len dropped a Pyrex bowl full of potatoes However, it was nice to eat chicken eggs and fresh meat for a change. The next day things improved. Sir Cosmo questioned me about the dogs at the span, and easily kept the conversation flowing. The Governor then left on the *Shackleton*. This ship finally relieved the three Fids who had been stranded on Detaille Island for six months. Other visitors were two orange USS *East Wind* navy turbo-helicopters. They photographed rather well outlined against the sky and the off-white snow.

Six days later the weather matched my low feelings. My time to leave on the *Biscoe* had come. I had run all eleven dogs for over eight miles the day before: I didn't feel like leaving just yet. But base life carried on. There was another large booze up, with the new people and the *Biscoe* crew including Peter Hay who was being demoted or promoted, depending on your viewpoint, from third officer on the *Biscoe* to fourth met man at Adelaide Island. He became a Fid by unintentionally stepping into the cold sea between the scow and the jetty. Next Peter and the second officer deliberately swam in the sea off the motorboat placed strategically by an iceberg. And I received one bottle of whisky from Roger for winning the 'is she or isn't she' pregnant Brownie bet.

Unloading with a three-year supply of food continued in case the Marguerite Bay sea ice became difficult again. On board ship that evening, the film *The Pumpkin Eaters* was only fair. But a big cheer went up when London Zoo penguins were spotted; we were not too sophisticated.

I had had my last sledge run and had fed the huskies. I was the unhappy one. The dogs now had someone else to look after them. I had appreciated the huskies' enthusiasm and energy during my two years in the Antarctic.

On January 30th bound for Stonington Island I boarded the Biscoe in sleet and in my own black cloud; more drinking took some of the edge off. At Stonington Island, teams from the one hundred available huskies moved supplies. Behind the base the ice ramp, a few hundreds yard in width, rose to the heavily crevassed Northeast Glacier. The glacier was the main route to the top of the Antarctic Peninsula, four to six thousand feet above Stonington.

Two days later Mac, Dennis, and Jim, a radar technician, were dropped off at North Guebriant Island, twelve miles east of Adelaide base. Three other people were placed on a second station on one of the Faure Islands, twenty miles south of Adelaide. *Biscoe* was to do hydrographical soundings of Marguerite Bay using the two radar slave stations as controls.

The initial two hours of the Hi-Fix programme of watching the depth sounder was interesting. Then it wasn't, especially in the slow early morning hours. The only diversion was the sudden change in the profile of the sea bottom when the depth would suddenly go from four hundred to twenty fathoms in a few boat lengths. Ship's officers moved fast under those conditions especially when a few rocks broke the surface of the water.

The large number of Stonington Island huskies needed a lot of seals. So we went sealing among the ice floes of Neny

Fjord, southeast of Stonington base. Tony Rider created a photographic moment by standing astride a splitting blood-spattered floe that the *Biscoe* had just rammed.

A return to boring Hi-Fix stints was only ameliorated by finally seeing the entire erotic *World of Suzie Wong*, which the Drake Passage storm had stopped us from seeing twenty-six months earlier. The rough weather of summer returned, as did my headiness, extra saliva, and use of seasick pills. John Noel and I climbed the 1700-foot Mt Searle on Horseshoe Island while the other Fids explored the closed-down base. John and I arrived back late, but the exercise was celebrated with three whiskies in the wardroom.

By the middle of February, I was thankfully deposited on land at the North Guebriant Island to replace Dennis.

35

Five Weeks of No Sailing

The North Guebriant Island lay four miles south off the Adelaide Island coast. It was four hundred yards long, and it attracted shiny white icebergs that drifted by. The closest bergs, if they had arches and holes, were photographed.

To the north of the small island projected the black Cape Alexandra; behind it rose the white-ridged mass of the 7,000-foot Mt Liotard, and to its right, the dark 1,800-foot cliffs of Jenny Island stood out from the lighter coloured sea. A six-foot high cairn at our highest point was used to focus on the distant mountains, and to add contrast to any reddened cloud-torn skies.

Living on the small island was Jim, the radar technician, for two months, a different Fid for two weeks stints, and myself for five weeks. The Fids included Mac, Davie Todd from Stonington Island, and Trevor Jones from the Argentine Islands. Some months earlier Davie, after breaking through sea ice, survived fifteen minutes in the water though five of his sledge dogs died. Trevor annoyed other Fids by being the only person to understand his radio messages from home; they were in Welsh. A variety of birds also lived on the island including skua chicks making careful flying circuits over the rocks. I climbed the 35-foot basalt cliffs around the edge of the isle, got fitter, and continued studying my physics and German.

We played cards, ate, drank, talked, and ragged Jim, the technician, about his girl friend, not that we were envious, mind you. After a month Jim had his first bath on HMS

Protector. One night I saw my first satellite heading north. The only live whales I saw during the whole of my stay in the Antarctic were two minkes, which sailed past the island.

I occasionally contemplated my lack of acuity. A fault of being young was being hard on one's self. I also had some lecherous thoughts though more toward Montevideo than Stanley. My sleeping libido was starting to awaken as the reality of leaving Antarctica emerged.

Back aboard the *Biscoe* the Antarctic leaving Fids celebrated, we dropped John Noel and others off at Stonington island base, and made a food depot at Snowshoe Glacier for next year's field teams.

The final Marguerite Bay event was the ascent of Jenny Island. Seven of us helped a navy-surveyor do a tellurometer reading from the top. Celebratory drinks were in order at the end of the day.

36

A Slow Boat to Southampton

The final eight weeks of my Antarctic life were a mixture of seasickness, boredom, restlessness, and the odd bit of interest. A couple of birthdays, including mine, led to crowded alcoholic cabin parties; some meteorological observations were missed. The two BAS ships separated for home with violent, colourful flares. I took more anti-seasick pills as we went up and down the Adelaide Island coast in sixty to seventy knot winds. On the radio we listened to the big election win by the Labour Party in Britain; the outside world was starting to encroach.

Mac, Jules and I retrieved our kitbags at Deception Island. We didn't linger. The new Fids wanted us on our way; they needed to experience their own Antarctica.

At Signy Island base in the South Orkney Islands we checked out the orange-plumed macaroni penguins and one irate fur seal that threatened to bite us. On the way to South Georgia, the *Biscoe's* second officer tried to bribe us with drinks to get one of us to replace Kenn Back as senior met man. For his third straight year down south Kenn had signed up for a year at South Georgia. There were no Fid takers on board ship as chief met man.

At South Georgia I stormed up Mt Hodges in an hour and a half, and came down in thirty minutes. We waved goodbye to Kenn, and headed for Stanley in the Falkland Islands. Roger Owen became chief met man, but he was *not* going to do observations. We were all getting a little stroppy as we adjusted to outside realities.

One Fid, who had been more difficult than most on a base that past winter, was being sent home. No one on his base could stand him.

I saw my last iceberg. It was a poignant reminder that for me the Antarctic was finished. Most Fids wouldn't see the southern ice again, though the memories would never leave us. The silences had contrasted with the sounds of blizzards. The isolation had brought us together, but also showed up our differences. The still white scenery left permanent images. And the huskies that responded to us, and gave more than they received, were remembered.

In Stanley the peat smoke smelled wonderful. I enjoyed seeing new people, cars, and flowers. I had my passport extended, three cavities in my teeth filled, and played badminton for three and a half hours.

There was a large Fid's party, and there were only three women there. Doreen smiled in recognition, but she had grown in stature and status. I didn't get a look in now. Worse, I had lost my wallet.

The next day we worked on putting up rhombic aerials for a link with the American base at McMurdo. I ate my first tripe and onions: interesting and chewy. I volunteered as a fullback in the Fids versus Stanley football game, and was then made centre forward. We lost one to three. The aerial work proceeded slowly despite Ted Clapp's threat that we would not be leaving unless the aerials were raised.

The next day had the usual blowing wind and rain. I noted I had another talk with Mrs Goodman at the dairy. I needed to talk to a woman. Then it was another hour and a half of fillings, and a loss at pair's badminton.

We left in rain the next day. Ian Barnes, the dentist, who had protected teeth in Stanley, now protected the rest of our bodies by handing out condoms as we entered Montevideo.

We hesitantly entered the routine of new foods and new, dark dingy bars in the large city. At El Patio I had thirteen-shilling (two-thirds of a pound) drinks and watched a strip show. These costly drinks saved me later at the Bonanza.

There Sherna and I examined my wallet. I was two hundred pesos short of the required price.

As the ban on eating meat on the weekend had finished, I went to the Victoria Plaza Hotel, and indulged in a vichyssoise soup, a Chateaubriand steak, and half a bottle of wine. In the afternoon I bought fruit, and that evening I overindulged at the Gruer Sur with shrimps, a flat fish, a chicken, and two cups of coffee after a bottle of Rhine wine. Fresh food was a higher priority than sex.

We bade farewell to Don Parnell doing a South American tour, and Davie Todd and Jimmy Gardner from Stonington Island on their Mt Aconcagua expedition. I felt like joining them. Our straight-up-the-Atlantic route, save for a distant glimpse of Recife in Brazil, entailed watching films of varying quality with our usual comments, painting the aft-deck, sunbathing, watching sheet lightning at night, and sleeping on deck. By the first week in May we were getting tired and restless. The remaining 1,500-mile journey seemed to have no end in sight.

The Bay of Biscay was calm, there were no films left to watch, more ships were around, the potatoes were finished, and the ice cream was the only food worth eating. On the seventeenth of May, the lights of the Isle of Wight blinked at us. The next day, home seemed imminent as we passed the *Queen Elizabeth*, and pointed our slow boat into Southampton harbour. Striking dockers took pity on us, and allowed us to land.

My feelings on reaching the UK, represented by Southampton, were more relief that the voyage was finished, than the emotions I felt about coming home. Over the past two years, home had been where ever I stayed. England would be my residence for a few months before I took off for Canada.

Disembarking took time. Some of the parents on the dock had tears for the return of their sons. The young men were caught between being young men who had independently survived two Antarctic years, and sons who would rather not now deal with family emotions. There were a few goodbyes between those of us who had been thrown together for an Antarctic winter or two. Then there was separation. We had finished with that part of our lives, and were moving on in new directions. There was not much to say; I stepped onto the dock.

My mother and I exchanged "Hellos," and a quick touch before we took my luggage to her car. We had rarely expressed our personal feelings so our muted greetings after two years absence were normal, but my mother was happy that I was back.

We adjusted to each other by talking about the British political and economic situation, on my mothers' side, and some censured incidents from the voyage, on my part. There were many new cars and new buildings on the way home. Borehamwood now had three betting shops, a Chinese restaurant, and one Wimpy Bar.

I adjusted to our house again, my room, and the dog and cat. In the garden late spring flowers bloomed under cool grey skies. I looked at everything intently to re-establish contact.

For the first few days I heard glacial ice calving and crashing into the sea as the French window's metal slider slid through its sleeve. On a friend's television huskies howled, and tears came to my eyes. The Antarctic "sounds" slowly faded away over the next few months.

I met up with friends. The comments ranged from giving me a semi-heroic status to befuddlement:

"Was it dangerous?'

"See many polar bears?"

"Why, for two years?"

I could answer little.

I visited my sister at her south Wales teaching college, and I had a bit of an "Antarctic explorer" status. There was a tentative connection with the pen pal Ann had introduced me to. Back in London I returned to work at Black's camping store for a month or two, and I studied for my physics and German exams. I slowly took in political events and figures, though I was in no rush to enter the "normal" world.

What had I accomplished? I had added to the meteorological knowledge of the world's fifth largest continent, which strongly impacted the world's weather. The climate changes that occurred over time, and were found from our data, were understood much later.

More important for me I had grown during my two Antarctic years. I socialized more, I was firmer in my decisions, and now I had goals to work towards. I could now answer my secondary school careers master about what I wanted to do in life.

I had experienced what most would never encounter or want to encounter. The Antarctic exerted a lifetime's influence on me: scenes, experiences, and conversations floated through my mind for many years. Once one left the ice, there were really only three choices: return to Antarctica, marry and settle down, or travel. I travelled to Canada.

In the next few years I diverted the allure of the frozen south by getting a university degree. Much of the degree was forgotten, unlike the Antarctic.

37

You Can Return

After my two years in the Antarctic I emigrated from the UK to Canada. There I married my wife Norma, obtained a couple of degrees, taught secondary school in central British Columbia for twenty-six years, and then retired. My CDs of Flanders and Swann and *Beyond the Fringe, Goon Show* tapes, and Bob Dylan and Limeliters' records were only faint reminders of long ago. My memories, the daily diaries, photographs, and writing this book brought the Antarctic back to the fore. Other Fids like Len and Don had done one more session in the Antarctic. Kenn ended up doing nine winter sessions, (one of which was at South Georgia), and six summer sessions; that was more than anyone else in the British Antarctic Survey. Jules kept on flying. Roger set up an Antarctic website, and Jim Wilson retired to Scotland. Jim Common still meets up with other ex-Fids. From his physiological studies of us Tom Davies moved into research.

Thirty-nine years after I left the Antarctic for good, I boarded the *Polar Star* in February 2005, and headed back to the Antarctic Peninsula, this time as a tourist. I flew to Vancouver, and the next day travelled to Los Angeles, Lima, Santiago, and a day later I was in Buenos Aires.

Buenos Aires had fewer English shops than in 1963. The street, Florida, was still jammed with pedestrians, crossing the sixteen lanes of Av. 9 de Julio was still an adventure, and the Argentinean beef was still delicious. From the Aeroparque, where Don, Tiny and I over forty years ago had slipped in from Montevideo, I flew to Ushuaia, 1,500 miles to the south.

Ushuaia, the southern most city in the world, sits on the north side of the Beagle Channel in Tierra del Fuego. From a frontier town with logging, farming, and until 1947, a prison, (now a museum for tourists), Ushuaia prospers with fishing in the winter, and a growing Antarctic tourist industry in the summer. The original small quaint board houses are being replaced with pseudo-alpine chalets and concrete and steel hotels; the only constant here is the steady westerly wind.

In the 1960's tourist ships rarely entered Antarctic waters. In 1969 Lars-Eric Linblad took the *Linblad Explorer*, built as an expeditionary cruise ship, to the Antarctic. The ship has made frequent trips to Antarctica; we met it twice on this trip as it carried passengers south.

In the 2003 to 2004 season more than thirty cruise ships, mostly from Ushuaia, headed south towards the Antarctic Peninsula. Our ship, the *Polar Star*, an icebreaker, nearly five times the size of either the *Shackleton* or the *John Biscoe*, was comfortably suited for aging Antarctic types, and was steered by a more reliable automatic system than using Fids. The cabins ranged from suites to three-bunk cabins. The ship had a wide observation lounge, a dining room, and a small gym that was a little difficult to use in rolling conditions. The library had deep comfortable leather chairs that were tied together to prevent them moving as the ship rolled; the ropes kept the sleeping, or reading, passengers secure.

Except for two of us, the passengers were all British. They soon had the ship's central heating turned down. Half the passengers had been on Antarctic bases from 1948 to the 1990's. All the ex-Fids except one were male, had less hair than earlier, (except on their eyebrows), more paunches, and there were a higher proportion of beards than in the general population. I knew a couple of the Fids from several decades back.

Though the old bases had had more support staff than scientists, the passengers on the *Polar Star* had a higher proportion of ex-scientists. There was also a higher ratio of doctors on board than in the general population. On this trip the Fid wives could hear other Fid stories, and see what their husbands had been talking about for all those years.

The expedition staff varied in nationality and expertise. One had skied from Russia to Canada via the North Pole. Another studied Arctic permafrost, another was a geologist, and two studied birds and whales. Some had mountaineered all over the world, and two others had worked with the British Antarctic Survey. The normal expeditionary slide presentations in the large-windowed lounge were out-numbered by the Fid slide shows ranging from "Detaille Island," "Crossing South Georgia" to "Dogs in Antarctica." One change was that there were fewer Fids propping up the bar late at night than in the old days.

The tone in the dining room at breakfast time was subdued. The noise level rose at lunch, and by the evening meal, was deafening, as everyone talked of the day's activities and the good old days. Having been away from the UK for a few decades I sometimes miscued on the different British accents.

During the sea voyage south to Marguerite Bay many of us were, or became, twitchers, noting every usual and unusual bird. Our list of prions, petrels, albatrosses, and other sea birds got longer and longer. Four decades earlier I had only seen two live whales. During the first few days on this trip I saw sei, humpback, and minke whales. Later, orcas were added to make over thirty sightings. Four of us saw a rare strap tooth whale making four leaps across our bow. (With age a lower tooth grows and straps itself over the whale's upper jaw).

Our first iceberg was spotted the modern way with GPS and satellite photographs. For much of the voyage our ship, with no keel, rolled sideways, sometimes as much as 20° either way. Then the passengers, ricocheted off the sides of the passageways, and the *Polar Star* dance took place as we rolled upstairs quickly, or found the stairs even steeper than usual. Some of the passengers had been on a Marguerite Bay Antarctic cruise in the year 2000, and had not reached Stonington Island. There was too much sea ice, and the ship was not an icebreaker. This trip our icebreaker had no sea ice to deal with.

38

Marguerite Bay Bases

Our first stop in Marguerite Bay was at Horseshoe Island, a small British base closed down in 1960. By now the air temperature was colder than the sea temperature. We edged down the ship's gangway to the bouncing zodiac boats, threaded our way through icebergs and ice chunks, and waded ashore on to a rocky beach. The painted walls of the old hut had been stripped by the winds; as two ex-Fids said, they had only painted these walls thirty-five years ago. Horseshoe Island base is #63 on the Antarctic Heritage Site list of over seventy Antarctic historical places.

Inside the small wooden hut the ex-Fids exclaimed over remembered Nansen sledge parts, seal meat hooks, rusty tins of Hunters Steak and Kidney Pie, tattered old books, coal stoves, sleeping bunks, and the store of Nutrican dog food.

We roamed the island, and encountered fur seals, rare for us from several decades ago. Mt Searle, which John Noel and I had climbed many years ago, like Mt Hodges later on in South Georgia, remained unclimbed on this trip; the tourist schedule did not allow for extraneous activities. Later in the observation lounge I apologized for the quality of the Hunter products. I mentioned my family's connection with the tins of meat. There was much applause, and several ex-Fids commented on their less than fond memories of these tinned delicacies.

At two closed down British bases around Marguerite Bay we waded ashore. At Rothera, on the southeast side of Adelaide Island, the *Polar Star* docked, and we strolled straight on to a concrete berth. Started in 1975, Rothera is the largest British Antarctic Survey base, and is the British science and logistics centre in the Antarctic Peninsula. The sciences are primarily atmospherics, glaciology, and biology. Only two tourist ships a season are allowed to interrupt the Rothera studies; we were the second.

A Dash 7 aircraft regularly flies in from the Falkland Islands, and lands on an all-weather 900-metre crushed-rock runway. This wheeled aircraft, carries up to sixteen passengers, and can land further south of Rothera on a blue ice site. Four ski-fitted Twin Otters fly 1,000 miles in to the Antarctic interior, and east to the Halley base, supplying scientific parties. Air travel makes a more abrupt arrival and departure to and from the Antarctic than sea travel.

Some twenty people winter at Rothera. In the summer several hundred more move in and out. A full time communications officer keeps the summer aircraft and science parties on track. A summer commander juggles the visitors' many demands. There are even a couple of domestic workers brought in to help keep the place tidy.

For us ex-Fids, the heavily mechanized Rothera was rather a different Antarctic base than what we were used to. Electricity, heating, and air-conditioning were supplied twenty-four hours a day. A reverse-osmosis system made fresh water out of seawater. Communications ranged from GPS, VHF, HF, Internet, e-mail, and satellite phones. Large well-equipped steel laboratories and accommodation blocks for eighty-eight people lay parallel to the runway. There were machines all around the base. A BAS Rothera diarist later wrote some of us "pioneers of Polar living were fascinated." I was interested in the base but not fascinated, though I certainly joined in the postcard buying "feeding frenzy." The Rothera doctor (as the postmaster) survived the tourist onslaught.

A major change for us was the removal of waste, both the current waste and ours of several years back. We used to throw our garbage into tidal cracks or just dump it. There was little disintegration in the cold conditions. We lacked foresight, and environmental laws were non-existent. Today no waste is thrown into the sea from ships or bases south of 60 degrees latitude.

The evening of our arrival, the Rothera personnel, many in their twenties, (they looked so young) wined and dined us, and they tried to understand where we had been, compared to where they were now. We made an effort to make sense of their regulated and regimented life. The UK headquarters had a lot more input into this base than it did to our more isolated bases of the past. The outside world could not be ignored as the daily e-mails poured in. Some Rothera personnel deliberately did not communicate home in order to have some semblance of an isolated Antarctic experience.

Unlike the old wooden Horseshoe Island base that had blended into the frozen landscape, Rothera base stood apart from the icy terrain. The personnel, especially in the summer, seemed to observe the Antarctic as if from afar rather than being part of it.

For meteorology I felt a bit superfluous as nowadays much of the weather is observed by automated weather stations costing 10,000-pounds sterling. They are cheaper to use, and don't drink booze. General field assistants now needed mechanical skills to run snowmobiles, as well as outdoor skills, plus social skills in order to deal with the many short-term summer scientists. The field tents were similar to ours, except for the solar panels keeping the radiophones charged up.

Present day BAS winterers sign on for only one year before applying for the second. There had been too many dropouts in recent years. Maybe we had fewer opportunities in our world than the present day Antarctic workers, so those of us who had signed on for two winters stayed on.

Women can now winter in the Antarctic. The BAS hierarchy in the past had been vehemently opposed to women wintering over. The Russians had women wintering in the Antarctic in the 1960's, the Americans in the 1970's, and even the Australians in the 1980's. Not until the mid-1990's were British women allowed to winter, despite UK anti-discrimination legislation.

The excuses were: the cost of altering buildings, men preferred having no women around, and there would be too much conflict. Sir Vivian Fuchs considered that women would break down base unity; they should just have their own all-women base.

The fact that women had often lived in cramped mountaineering conditions with men for long periods of time was ignored. BAS belied its scientific impartiality by blatantly keeping women out of the Antarctic.

Five women on the *Polar Star*, though qualified, had all been turned down by BAS in the past. One was told: "BAS does not hire women." Now women are courted to go south, especially in the technical and physicist areas. New policies, and possible litigation, are keeping BAS politically correct.

Another initial British reluctance in the Antarctic was using huskies. Man hauling was the British way; using dogs was "going native." The British Graham Land Expedition, (1934 to 1937), and Operation Tabarin during the Second World War altered the earlier attitudes. Huskies became the main transportation in the British Antarctic for thirty years.

With more aircraft and efficient snowmobiles in the 1970's and 1980's, huskies were culled. By 1991 even without the Environmental Protocol, British Antarctic huskies were no longer used for sledging. The environmental pressures and regulations didn't allow any foreign species in Antarctic territory. The huskies, though they had all been born in the Antarctic, were considered alien, and were removed by 1994. The last twelve dogs from the Huns and Admirals teams were taken to the Canadian Arctic. After fifty years of isolation, most of the transplanted huskies succumbed to viral infections. The huskies had left a small imprint (sic!) in the Antarctic, and that had now gone.

The Environmental Protocol said nothing about the main foreign species in the Antarctic, humans, and their machinery. Several thousand people study the "national reserve devoted to science" in the Antarctic summer. Most do not consider the human impact, including the more than twenty-seven thousand tourists a year, as environmentally harmful; and now the rest of the world's pollution, by air and sea, is being deposited on Antarctica.

What has changed for the present day British Antarctic Survey personnel is the increase in fire, search and rescue, and field training. Personnel are trained in the UK, and then have a three-day off-base camping and crevasse rescue sessions in the snow and ice. Spur of the moment trips are not permitted. The death rate in the last thirty years has been about a third of what ours was. Sea ice travel is restricted, and there is more air support.

There were, however, several crosses at Rothera for the 1958 Dion Island party, for two crevasse deaths in 1981, for four who died in a plane crash in 1994, and in 2003, for Kirsty Brown, a biologist, who was drowned by a leopard seal. Kirsty's parents were courageous enough to be on the *Polar Star* cruise to visit the place where their daughter had died.

Our next Marguerite Bay stop was Stonington Island a small rocky island next to the Northeast Glacier. A fresh covering of snow covered the rocks and any human debris. There was a rush to photograph a juvenile Emperor penguin just off shore, followed by a rather sombre pilgrimage to John Noel and Tom Allan's cross.

A week after I arrived back in the UK in 1966, John and Tom took a sledging trip, and were caught in a katabatic wind sweeping down from the plateau above. From their snow hole, Tom went out unroped and did not return. John stayed at the entrance calling for him. They were both found frozen to death. Their two chained-up dog teams had drowned under the snow. On our trip Neil Marsden, one of the two who had found them, stood silently by the white cross.

The rest of the morning we tramped through sparkling snow photographing the old American hut, now iced in, and the better-preserved British hut. Both are Antarctic heritage sites. The Northeast Glacier's end ramp, that once had over a hundred huskies spanned on it, was gone. The snout of the glacier had receded, and we could now see and photograph Adelaide Island some sixty miles away.

As the *Polar Star* left Stonington, many old Fids recaptured old memories by dangling themselves over the ship's bow to photograph small ice floes being splintered. The *Polar Star* sailed across the sparkling Marguerite Bay with whales and penguins surfacing close by; to the east the white Antarctic Peninsula shone in the sunshine. Jenny Island's 1,800 foot cliffs rose from the dimpled sea, North Guebriant Island, where I had spent five weeks camping, appeared, and behind it projected the black Cape Alexandra and the white Ditte and Liotard Mountains. Avian Island swarmed with birds, but no humans. The island is now a "specially protected area," one of 150 sites, mostly on the Antarctic Peninsula. Behind Avian Island the long flat Adelaide Island glacier swept along the southern coast.

As the wind came up only those who had previously been on the Adelaide Island base were allowed to attempt the landing. Ice Berg Alley lived up to its name as we dodged large mountains of ice in the rising sea. Most of the old base huts were still visible on the rocks. Hampton House had been taken to Rothera. On the skyline was the remains of the orange fuselage of the crashed Otter '377'. The other Otter of my day had been taken to the de Haviland Aircraft Heritage Centre in the UK.

Several fur seals cavorted among the rocks and in the sea. We had seen none in the 1960's. I continuously photographed Adelaide Island base, but we didn't get any closer to the landing site as the waves rose higher. As the tourist is a commodity, the expedition could not afford to lose any between the wet rocks and the moving boats. We retreated leaving the island untouched.

39

Southern Isles

The *Polar Star* adhered to its tourist itinerary, and in sleeting rain took us two hundred miles north of the Adelaide Island base to the Argentine Islands. Surrounding ice prevented us from visiting the Ukrainians' base of Vernadsky, previously the British base on the Argentine Islands. We made do with peering in at the old British Wordie Hut, another Historic Site, on Winter Island just opposite where the Ukrainians carried on upper atmospheric studies.

We then moved through the narrow scenic Lemaire Channel. Rocky buttresses and hanging glaciers rose on either side, but with low grey cloud there were few pictures taken except for the occasional Weddell and leopard seal, and porpoising penguins.

At Paradise Bay at the closed down Argentinean base of Almirante Brown, we slid down a snowy hillside on our upside down life jackets; it was like wearing adult diapers. We photographed moulting gentoo penguins, a resting crabeater seal on an ice floe, a high cracked glacier snout, and another zodiac seen through an arch in an iceberg.

The Port Lockroy base visit, (a refurbished historic site), with BAS personnel selling souvenirs to the tourists, (there had to be one Antarctic tourist trap), and a successful landing rate of 97% for other tourist ships, was aborted. The afternoon brought high winds and waves. Bill Bailey at age 82 had been at Port Lockroy in 1948, but didn't get to land this time. Unlike in our day, there were sailing yachts anchored at Port Lockroy. In two days we had seen seven vessels including the sailing ship, *Europa*. In the summer the Antarctic Peninsula is no longer a pristine place empty of humans, rather to the disappointment of some visitors. Though the latest 2002 charts of the coast still include large areas that are unsurveyed.

A day later we landed at Deception Island with low cloud enveloping the mountaintops. Change was obvious here, and not only due to global warming. (The only two Antarctic flowering plants, hair grass and pearlwort, had increased rapidly on Deception and elsewhere). Deception's first flush toilet, installed in 1965 the year that I was at Adelaide, lasted just over two years. The Deception Island November 1967 earth tremors, led in December to a huge venting of ash and gas near the Chilean base. As volcanic ash rained down, the Chileans fled to the British base in the dark, and by the next morning Chilean helicopters had evacuated every one off the island. The British returned in '68, but in February '69 more eruptions occurred. Fortunately, as with the previous occasion, the volcanic eruptions happened in the summer time. At present volcanic studies are only carried out in summer at an Argentinean and a Spanish base. Deception Island no longer has permanent Antarctic bases for political positioning.

We landed at Whalers Bay beach among sporting young dark grey fur seals; I saw only one forty years ago. I hurriedly walked ahead of the other passengers towards my old base across the black ash, strewn with newer orange ash deposits. Four rusty whale oil tanks remained; most of the whaling factory had disappeared though the Fidase hut was in a reasonable good condition. Two crosses had been resurrected. Most of the whalers' graveyard was buried under volcanic ash.

Biscoe House, my home for fourteen months, lay abandoned with a gaping hole in its centre where mud and ash had poured through. I could look through the bar area to the *Polar Star* beyond. I climbed rickety stairs to the Green Room where Don, Charles, and I had slept. There was nothing left of any consequence now. The "new" green plastic hut's foundations were still showing, but the hut was not. It had disappeared just before 1986; this time the agency was human.

I visited the abandoned hangar. On the beach the former multitudinous whalebone vertebrae were mostly covered with ash; only a few broken casks and the odd whaleboat poked through the black surface. Deception Island did not have anything left that I could hold on to.

I peered over Neptunes Window to the sea below. Here I had had to put Saki down. I returned to the beach, and had a rapid wade in a man- made disintegrating hot pool. Others from our ship had an Antarctic "swim" earlier. I was the last person to climb into the returning zodiac. I hadn't felt like talking to many people that day. Sometimes one cannot go home again.

In misty cloud and more wind a second ship sailed past us to the north end of Port Foster. There are few scientists on Deception Island, but it is the most heavily visited tourist place in Antarctica. Where else can you sail into a volcanic caldera that might still erupt? There had been further eruptions in 1970, and the early 1990's.

As we left I could see the breach that allowed the sea to enter Kroner Lake. I didn't see the wrecked *Southern Hunter* in Neptunes Bellows. I tried to hold images of Deception Island in my mind as we steamed away. Outside, in the distance, bits of Baily Head could be seen disappearing into cloud.

On the moss-covered, wet, ex-volcanic South Shetland Island of Aitcho ("H.O.") elderly *Polar Star* passengers met frisky young fur seals, placid young elephant seals, and young gentoo and chinstrap penguins. The Environmental Protocol rule of keeping five metres away from wildlife was difficult to apply when a penguin came up close, and with its beak tapped your leg. Two different young fur seals bit two different passengers. Antibiotics were administered. Back on board ship, by stepping into a tray of disinfectant, we at least did not transmit any pathogens from one landing site to another.

In true tourist fashion the *Polar Star* rushed to keep up with its schedule. The long distances meant that half of our twenty-day trip was sea travel. More pills and patches were needed as we ploughed through rolling seas past a wet and windy Elephant Island, where Sir Ernest Shackleton had brought his twenty-seven men in 1916, after the Endurance had been crushed by the sea ice of the Weddell Sea.

A chest virus got to half the passengers and crew. Those of us who remained healthy photographed wildlife, and the many wave-beaten and cave-sculptured icebergs. Some bergs were tabular and up to five miles long. These had broken off the Larsen Ice Shelf on the east side of the Antarctic Peninsula. On the Peninsula 87 % of the glaciers had retreated in the last fifty years. In that time the region's temperature had risen on an average by 2.5 degrees C.

Some of us still used film in our cameras. Most people clicked and deleted with digital cameras. Charts in the bridge were "filmed," including the one that showed an ocean depth east of the South Sandwich Island of 8,323 metres. I later felt that my camera came between the Antarctic and myself. I could not return to what had been, but by leaving the camera closed I could at least experience as much as possible with out this distraction.

Early morning winds of up to 60 knots with spume whipping off the wave tops prevented a Signy Island base landing in the South Orkney Islands. We missed the British personnel's refreshments. At Orcadas, the oldest continuously manned Antarctic base that the Argentineans had acquired in 1904, the steady westerly wind stopped us from landing as well.

We were now north of the Weddell Sea. 900 miles south of us at 75° 31′ was Halley Bay. It had lost its icy end pieces, and was today just called Halley. To avoid burial from the 1.2 metre yearly snow accumulation the fifth base is on stilts that can be jacked up. The new sixth base will also be kept above the snow.

Studies from Halley and Faraday, (the later name for the Argentine Islands base), had the first confirmations in 1985 that the ozone layer was weakening. Ionospheric and glacial measuring continue at Halley, as does the June 21st measuring of a different sort when the inhabitants of Halley run naked around the Laws Building at whatever the low winter temperature is that day.

Near South Georgia the wind lessened, the sun shone on a burnished steel ocean, and the wildlife increased as the icebergs were left behind. The air temperature was now warmer than the sea. The residents on the black shingle beach of Gold Harbour of moulting elephant seals, gentoo penguins, bellicose teenage fur seals, and hundreds of stately black, white, and orange and yellow-blotched king penguins mixed with the incoming travellers. The king penguins are eight inches shorter than the more well known emperor penguins, and less than half their weight.

In East Cumberland Bay, Grytviken was now a deserted and derelict whaling station. The British government has spent a lot of money on removing the buildings' asbestos. There was little left to show of what the main South Georgia industry used to be. We visited Shackleton's grave and the local museum, and rang the bells at the 1913 wooden church. My cabin mate, Ian, and I came back later to the gravesite to get photographs uninterrupted by the hordes of other passengers. The clumps of snorting, coughing, blinking, tearful, wallowing elephant seals, a favourite of mine, were also photographed.

In the afternoon we had high tea at the BAS fishing research base of King Edward Point, and that evening we hosted an outside barbeque on the *Polar Star's* aft deck for the BAS personnel.

Further along the coast at Fortuna Bay we saw the same wildlife as at Gold Harbour plus the added attraction of semi-wild reindeer. Norwegian whalers had brought them in for fresh meat at the beginning of the last century. By going on a hike towards the Koenig Glacier I missed a well-digitalized leopard seal minding its own business on a nearby beach.

In the afternoon we set off on the "Long March." In 1916, having arrived at the south side of South Georgia, Shackleton set off with Worsley and Crean to cross twenty-two miles of unknown mountains and glaciers to the north side of the island to get help for his men stranded on Elephant Island, some 800 miles away. Above Fortuna Bay they heard the 7 o'clock morning Stromness whaling factory whistle, near the end of their thirty-six hour winter slog. Few people have duplicated the whole trip, even in summer time.

Most of the *Polar Star* passengers duplicated the final few miles of the trio's trek. We came down from the 1,000-foot col to Stromness, now deserted, save for hundreds of young fur seals frolicking on the beach and in and out of the run-down wooden and galvanized buildings. The seals ignored the asbestos notice warnings.

We next went to Prion Island in the Bay of Isles to observe nesting wandering albatrosses. There would be a flurry of activity from the humans as a young albatross, (the top of the wings were still black), waddled through the tussac grass, and slowly launched itself into the wind. The wide-winged bird would then sail away on the air currents.

After lunch we landed at Salisbury Plain where 40,000 king penguins stood around in a massed group. A few still wore the chick's chocolate-brown feathery fuzz. From the top of a nearby hill the penguins looked like the cast of thousands from a 1950's film epic.

The Falkland Islands were our final southern isles stop, reached after two days of a plunging rolling sea voyage. I was looking forward to ending the unrelenting sea travel, though I was not interested in outside world affairs. The temporary isolation was a holiday in itself.

Black and white Peale's dolphins played on our bow wave as we approached the entrance to Stanley Harbour. The surrounding flat scenery looked the same though the town of Stanley had doubled in area since my last visit forty years ago. Half of the Falkland's population used to live outside of Stanley. Now most live in the capital. The security card handed to us on the dock was a change from the old relaxed days, as were the paved roads, the stream of four-wheel drive vehicles, the TV aerials, and new buildings such as the leisure centre. Stanley was no longer a backwater of the British Empire.

There were a few remaining evocative peat stove smells; however, oil furnaces were now more convenient. Sheep still dominated the landscape, but fishing and fish licenses drove the economy. The locals were in touch with the rest of the world's culture; the standard of living had risen.

The local museum exhibited the history of the Falkland Islands with the last major display being the ten-week war with Argentina in 1982. The war brought money, improved infrastructures, a large airstrip, and a continuing military presence to the Falkland Islands. In the 1960's and 1970's the British, against the wishes of the locals, tried to give the islands to the Argentineans. Now the British were dug in for the long haul. In 1983 science benefitted from this conflict by seeing the BAS budget jump by 60%. Political status in the Antarctic still has some importance.

Reminders of the war were the fenced off beach areas around Stanley that were still mined, and the large new war memorial. The memorial had 255 names of the British dead, including three Falkland Islanders accidentally shelled by the Royal Navy. In Ushuaia on a large display by the coast, the Argentineans had a memorial to their 1200 dead. For Argentina the Islas Malvinas (the Falkland Islands) are not forgotten.

The last stop on our southern itinerary was West Point Island in the far west of the Falkland Islands. In a high biting wind we photographed nesting black-browed albatrosses mingling with yellow-tufted rockhopper penguins. Some of the black-browed albatrosses have been measured gliding 8,000 kilometres to Brazil and back to gather food for their young. Albatrosses are declining in numbers each year. They eat the fish-baited hooks on the mile long fishing lines of the Southern Ocean. We sailed past New Island South, another wildlife reserve, due to the continuing high winds. High winds had curtailed a third of our planned stops.

In winds up to 70-knots we headed for South America. Scores of albatrosses skimmed in our wake; they turned on the tips of waves and disappeared behind rising swells.

Early in the morning at Ushuaia we disembarked from the *Polar Star*, as the crew and staff prepared for the next lot of passengers headed for the southern Antarctic isles.

40

One Antarctic Ending

We ex-Fids appreciated the modern conveniences of Rothera in Marguerite Bay, and King Edward Point at South Georgia - no coal heating and no melting snow. But we felt that the "real" Antarctica had disappeared. Roughing it had been part of the adventure for us down south.

When we eighty or so young men had left for the Antarctic in 1963, it was an exciting time only available to a fortunate few. Today, increased media coverage, new technologies, a hundred years of interest in the Antarctic, and the challenge of finding experiences that are different from others in the world has led to an "invasion" of this remote frozen continent. The cold, the wind, the isolation and the logistical difficulties still restrict the numbers of people getting there, but the attraction of the Antarctic is increasing.

Just as you can be guided up Mount Everest if you have the financial means so the unique icy and pristine Antarctic is open to anyone with sufficient finances. In the Antarctic one can sightsee, swim, (one woman swam a mile in the frigid Antarctic seas), kayak, yacht, ski, mountaineer, scuba dive, and run marathons. In 2005, 176 runners completed the King George Island Antarctic marathon in the South Shetland Islands. At a greater price one can run the colder marathon of 26.2 miles, on the mainland.

Crossing the Antarctic is now a competition in categories of gender, age, and method. To get to the South Pole and beyond some people walk, some ski, and some are blown by kites. No one has crossed the Antarctic in mid-winter, but it will only be a matter of time.

From my earlier Antarctic adventure I have a few regrets. Why did I not try a polar swim off Adelaide, or eat boiled krill from the low tide on Deception Island's beach? Hindsight showed that if Tom Miller and I had tried to climb Mt Bouvier it could have been fatal. Then who would have looked after the huskies? As a hairy winterer I was fond of the huskies. Their absence diminishes the Antarctic.

On this trip the limitations of being a tourist in the Antarctic lessened its fascination for me. Most Antarctic tourist travel is spent on water. There is little time spent on solid ice or rock as one moves from selected site to selected site on an ongoing itinerary. There is limited input and choice, so on a personal level the effect of the Antarctic is lessened.

I was, however, grateful to be part of the *Polar Star* cruise even if it could not bring back the golden years. For the thousands working in Antarctica this present time will be *their* golden age compared to future generations. Antarctica has approximately 4,000 scientists and support staff working each summer. From twelve signatories to the Antarctic Treaty in 1961, there are now some twenty-seven countries with forty or so permanent bases in the Antarctic. The exact number varies from year-to-year depending on economic consid-erations. King George Island, a hundred and twenty miles northeast of Deception Island, has eight different countries with eight different permanent bases situated on it. The Antarctic Peninsula region is, and will be, taking most of the environmental pressure from humans in science and travel.

A few want to keep the Antarctic as a pristine science laboratory. But the tourist tide to the Antarctic is increasing. In the 1995 to 1996 season 9,061 people visited the Antarctic. Ten years later the number has tripled. The majority of travellers head to the more accessible Antarctic Peninsula. Most organi-zations belong to the International Association of Antarctic Tour Operators that monitors and promotes safe environ-mental travel in Antarctica. The concern is not so much from large cruise ships that do not land passengers, but from smaller one- hundred passenger ships that make several landings for each cruise during the November to March season. Nesting birds can be vulnerable to intruders. Limiting the number of sites and the frequency of landing is promoted. The increasing traffic to the Antarctic will be a concern in the future.

Everyone in the Antarctic, whether down for a three-week trip or for repeat seasons as a scientist, is in a sense a visitor. All fuel and food must be brought in; no one can live off the Antarctic. It is a continent on which humans have made the least impact. But Antarctica leaves an impression on those who visit it. Some use the Antarctic to reflect their own philosophical or metaphysical thoughts and feelings. Each person brings away his or her own reactions to this frozen white continent. To paraphrase Wilfred Thesiger on the deserts in *Arabian Sands*, the harsh Antarctic casts a spell, which milder climes cannot compete with. Antarctica is unique. Humans can only take this uniqueness away in their minds.

Bibliography

A few pertinent books on the past and the present Antarctic:

Fuchs, Sir Vivian. *Of Ice and Men*. Oswestry: Anthony Nelson, 1982

Ommanney, F.D. *South Latitude*. London, Longmans, Green and Co, 1938

Pearce, Cliff. *The Silent Sound*. Sussex: The Book Guild, 2004

Rubin, Jeff. *Antarctica*. 3rd ed. Oakland, CA: Lonely Planet Publications Pty Ltd, 2005

Rymill, John. *Southern Lights*. London: Harper and Brothers Publishers, 1939

Walton, Kevin and Atkinson, Rick. *Of Dogs and Men*. Malvern: Image Publishing, 1996

Biography

Michael grew up in Britain. After working in a store he joined the British Antarctic Survey as a meteorologist. After one year at Deception Island and one year at Adelaide Island he moved to Canada. He married Norma, and taught secondary school for twenty-six years in central British Columbia. Now retired, he runs marathons, writes, and gardens. He belongs to the British Antarctic Survey Club, the American Polar Society, and the New Zealand Antarctic Society. You can find Michael's website articles under "Michael Warr Antarctic."

For more copies of *South of Sixty*:

Email: mwarr@telus.net *(North America)*
Awarr@btinternet.com *(UK)*

www.antarcticmemoriespublishing.com